British Railways Pocket B

CO
ST__CK

FORTY-FOURTH EDITION
2020

The complete guide to all
Locomotive-Hauled Carriages which
operate on the national railway network

Robert Pritchard

PLATFORM
5

ISBN 978 1909 431 55 3

© 2019. Platform 5 Publishing Ltd, 52 Broadfield Road, Sheffield, S8 0XJ,
England.

Printed in England by The Lavenham Press, Lavenham, Suffolk.

CONTENTS

PROVISION OF INFORMATION

This book has been compiled with care to be as accurate as possible, but some information is not easily available and the publisher cannot be held responsible for any errors or omissions. We would like to thank the companies and individuals who have been helpful in supplying information to us. The authors of this series of books are always pleased to receive notification of any inaccuracies that may be found, to enhance future editions. Please send comments to:

Robert Pritchard, Platform 5 Publishing Ltd, 52 Broadfield Road, Sheffield, S8 0XJ, England.

e-mail: robert.pritchard@platform5.com   **Tel:** 0114 255 2625.

This book is updated to information received by 11 October 2019.

UPDATES

This book is updated to the Stock Changes given in **Today's Railways UK 215** (November 2019). The Platform 5 railway magazine "**Today's Railways UK**" publishes Stock Changes every month to update this book. The magazine also contains news and rolling stock information on the railways of Great Britain and Ireland and is published on the second Monday of every month. For further details of **Today's Railways UK**, please contact Platform 5 Publishing Ltd.

Front cover photograph: CrossCountry-liveried HST Trailer Standard 42377, fitted with sliding doors, is seen near Rotherham on 06/06/19. **Robert Pritchard**

BRITAIN'S RAILWAY SYSTEM

INFRASTRUCTURE & OPERATION

Britain's national railway infrastructure is owned by a "not for dividend" company, Network Rail. In 2014 Network Rail was reclassified as a public sector company, being described by the Government as a "public sector arm's-length body of the Department for Transport".

Most stations and maintenance depots are leased to and operated by Train Operating Companies (TOCs), but some larger stations are controlled by Network Rail. The only exception is the infrastructure on the Isle of Wight: The Island Line franchise uniquely included maintenance of the infrastructure as well as the operation of passenger services. As Island Line is now part of the South Western Railway franchise, both the infrastructure and trains are operated by South Western Railway.

Trains are operated by TOCs over Network Rail tracks (the National Network), regulated by access agreements between the parties involved. In general, TOCs are responsible for the provision and maintenance of the locomotives, rolling stock and staff necessary for the direct operation of services, whilst Network Rail is responsible for the provision and maintenance of the infrastructure and also for staff to regulate the operation of services.

The Department for Transport (DfT) is the franchising authority for the national network, with Transport Scotland overseeing the award of the ScotRail franchise and the Welsh Government overseeing the Wales & Borders franchise.

A franchise is the right to run specified services within a specified area for a period of time, in return for the right to charge fares and, where appropriate, to receive financial support from the Government. Subsidy is payable in respect of socially necessary services. Service standards are monitored by the DfT throughout the duration of the franchise. Franchisees earn revenue primarily from fares and from subsidy. They generally lease stations from Network Rail and earn rental income by sub-letting parts of them, for example to retailers.

TOC's and open access operator's main costs are the track access charges they pay to Network Rail, the costs of leasing stations and rolling stock and of employing staff. Franchisees may do light maintenance work on rolling stock or contract it out to other companies. Heavy maintenance is normally carried out by the Rolling Stock Leasing Companies, according to contracts.

TOCs can take commercial risks, although some franchises are "management contracts", where ticket revenues pass directly to the DfT. Concessions (such as London Overground) see the operator paid a fee to run the service, usually within tightly specified guidelines. Operators running a concession would not normally take commercial risks, although there are usually penalties and rewards in the contract.

Note that a railway "reporting period" is four weeks.

DOMESTIC PASSENGER TRAIN OPERATORS

The majority of passenger trains are operated by Train Operating Companies on fixed-term franchises or concessions. Expiry dates are shown in the list below:

Franchise	Franchisee	Trading Name
Caledonian Sleeper	Serco (until 31 March 2030)	**Caledonian Sleeper**

This franchise started in April 2015 when operation of the ScotRail and ScotRail Sleeper franchises was separated. Abellio won the ScotRail franchise and Serco the Caledonian Sleeper franchise. Caledonian Sleeper operates four trains nightly between London Euston and Scotland using locomotives hired principally from GBRf. New CAF Mark 5 rolling stock is currently being introduced, replacing the old Mark 2 and Mark 3 stock – due to be fully retired in autumn 2019.

Chiltern	Arriva (Deutsche Bahn) (until 11 December 2021)	**Chiltern Railways**

There is an option to extend the franchise by 7 months to July 2022.

Chiltern Railways operates a frequent service between London Marylebone, Oxford, Banbury and Birmingham Snow Hill, with some peak trains extending to Kidderminster. There are also regular services from Marylebone to Stratford-upon-Avon and to Aylesbury Vale Parkway via Amersham (along the London Underground Metropolitan Line). The fleet consists of DMUs of Classes 165, 168 and 172 plus a number of locomotive-hauled rakes used on some of the Birmingham and Oxford route trains, worked by Class 68s hired from DRS.

Cross Country	Arriva (Deutsche Bahn) (until 17 October 2020)	**CrossCountry**

In 2018 competition for the next franchise was stopped, pending the publication of a Rail Review by the Government.

CrossCountry operates a network of long distance services between Scotland, the North-East of England and Manchester to the South-West of England, Reading, Southampton, Bournemouth and Guildford, centred on Birmingham New Street. These trains are mainly formed of diesel Class 220/221 Voyagers, supplemented by a small number of HSTs on the NE–SW route. Inter-urban services also link Nottingham, Leicester and Stansted Airport with Birmingham and Cardiff. These trains use Class 170 DMUs.

Crossrail	MTR (until 27 May 2023)	**TfL Rail**

There is an option to extend the concession by 2 years to May 2025.

This is a new concession which started in May 2015. Initially Crossrail took over the Liverpool Street–Shenfield stopping service from Greater Anglia, using a fleet of Class 315 EMUs, with the service branded "TfL Rail". New Class 345 EMUs are being introduced on this route and are also used between Paddington and Hayes & Harlington (both initially in 7-car formation). The Hayes services will be extended to Reading with 9-car sets from December 2019. TfL Rail currently also operates the former Heathrow Connect stopping service that uses Class 360 EMUs. The opening of Crossrail through central London has been delayed and operation through new tunnels beneath central London, from Shenfield and Abbey Wood in the east to Reading and Heathrow Airport in the west is now expected between October 2020 and March 2021. It will then be branded the "Elizabeth Line".

East Coast   **London North Eastern Railway**

Franchise awarded to Stagecoach/Virgin Trains in 2015 but was terminated just over 3 years later in 2018 (having originally been due to operate until 2023) after the franchise failed. Currently operated on an interim basis by the DfT's "Operator of Last Resort". It is due to be relet in the future as part of a new public/private East Coast partnership.

LNER operates frequent long distance trains on the East Coast Main Line between London King's Cross, Leeds, York, Newcastle-upon-Tyne and Edinburgh, with less frequent services to Bradford, Harrogate, Skipton, Hull, Lincoln, Glasgow, Stirling, Aberdeen and Inverness. The former BR Class 91 + Mark 4 and HST fleets are currently being phased out as a new fleet of 65 Hitachi Class 800 and 801 "Azuma" trains are introduced (these are a mix of bi-mode and electric, 5- and 9-car units). The Azumas are all due to be in traffic by June 2020.

East Midlands   Abellio   **East Midlands Railway**
                                (until 21 August 2027)
There is an option to extend the franchise by 2 years to August 2029.

EMR operates a mix of long distance high speed services on the Midland Main Line (MML), from London St Pancras to Sheffield (to Leeds at peak times and with some extensions to York/Scarborough), Nottingham (plus peak-hour trains to Lincoln) and Corby, and local and regional services ranging from the long distance Norwich–Liverpool route to Nottingham–Skegness, Nottingham–Mansfield–Worksop, Newark–Matlock and Derby–Crewe. It also operates local services in Lincolnshire. Trains on the MML are worked by a fleet of Class 222 DMUs and 12 HSTs, whilst the local and regional fleet consists of DMU Classes 153, 156 and 158.

East Anglia   Abellio (Netherlands Railways) (60%)/Mitsui Group (40%)   **Greater Anglia**
                                (until 11 October 2025)
There is an option to extend the franchise by 1 year to October 2026.

Greater Anglia operates main line trains between London Liverpool Street, Ipswich and Norwich and local trains across Norfolk, Suffolk and parts of Cambridgeshire. It also runs local and commuter services into Liverpool Street from the Great Eastern (including Southend, Braintree and Clacton) and West Anglia (including Ely/Cambridge and Stansted Airport) routes. It operates a varied fleet of Class 90s with locomotive-hauled Mark 3 sets, DMUs of Classes 153, 156 and 170 and EMUs of Classes 317, 321, 360 and 379. The first of a completely new fleet of trains (Class 755 bi-mode units) were introduced in summer 2019, and new trains (Classes 720, 745 and 755) will be introduced across all routes by 2021.

Essex Thameside   Trenitalia   **c2c**
                                (until 10 November 2029)
There is an option to extend the franchise by 6 months to May 2030.

c2c operates an intensive, principally commuter, service from London Fenchurch Street to Southend and Shoeburyness via both Upminster and Tilbury. The fleet consists of 74 Class 357 EMUs, plus six Class 387s.

Great Western   First Group   **Great Western Railway**
                         (until 31 March 2020)
Direct Award extension expected to March 2022, with the option of a further 2 year extension to March 2024.

Great Western Railway operates long distance trains from London Paddington to South Wales, the West Country and Worcester and Hereford. In addition there are frequent trains along the Thames Valley corridor to Newbury/Bedwyn and Oxford, plus local and regional trains throughout the South-West including the Cornish, Devon and Thames Valley branches, the Reading–Gatwick

North Downs Line and Cardiff–Portsmouth Harbour and Bristol–Weymouth regional routes. Long distance services are now in the hands of a new fleet of Class 800/802 bi-mode InterCity Express Trains. DMUs of Classes 165 and 166 are used on the Thames Valley branches and North Downs routes as well as on local services around Bristol and across to Cardiff. Class 387 EMUs are used between Paddington, Reading, Didcot Parkway and Newbury. Classes 143, 150 and 158 and a fleet of short 4-car HSTs are used on local and regional trains in the South-West. A small fleet of Class 57s is maintained to work the overnight "Cornish Riviera" Sleeper service between London Paddington and Penzance formed of Mark 3 coaches.

| **London Rail** | Arriva (Deutsche Bahn) (until 25 May 2024) | **London Overground** |

This is a concession and is different from other rail franchises, as fares and service levels are set by Transport for London instead of by the DfT. There is an option to extend the concession by 2 years to May 2026.

London Overground operates services on the Richmond–Stratford North London Line and the Willesden Junction–Clapham Junction West London Line, plus the East London Line from Highbury & Islington to New Cross and New Cross Gate, with extensions to Clapham Junction (via Denmark Hill), Crystal Palace and West Croydon. It also runs services from London Euston to Watford Junction. All these use Class 378 EMUs, with new Class 710s currently being introduced on the Watford route. Class 710s also now operate services on the Gospel Oak–Barking line. London Overground also operates some suburban services from London Liverpool Street – to Chingford, Enfield Town and Cheshunt. These use Class 315 and 317 EMUs, but are to be replaced by Class 710s in 2019–20.

| **Merseyrail Electrics** | Serco (50%)/Abellio (Netherlands Railways) (50%) (until 22 July 2028) | **Merseyrail** |

Under the control of Merseytravel PTE instead of the DfT. Franchise reviewed every five years to fit in with the Merseyside Local Transport Plan.

Merseyrail operates services between Liverpool and Southport, Ormskirk, Kirkby, Hunts Cross, New Brighton, West Kirby, Chester and Ellesmere Port, using Class 507 and 508 EMUs. A new fleet of Class 777 EMUs will be introduced in 2020–21.

| **Northern** | Arriva (Deutsche Bahn) (until 31 March 2025) | **Northern** |

There is an option to extend the franchise by 1 year to March 2026.

Northern operates a range of inter-urban, commuter and rural services throughout the North of England, including those around the cities of Leeds, Manchester, Sheffield, Liverpool and Newcastle. The network extends from Chathill in the north to Nottingham in the south, and Cleethorpes in the east to St Bees in the west. Long distance services include Leeds–Carlisle, Morpeth–Carlisle and York–Blackpool North. The operator uses a large fleet of DMUs of Classes 142, 144, 150, 153, 155, 156, 158, 170 and 195 plus EMU Classes 319, 321, 322, 323, 331 and 333. The new fleets of DMUs (Class 195) and EMUs (Class 331) are now being introduced on a number of routes, and will be followed by Class 769 bi-mode diesel electric units (converted from Class 319s). Most of the Class 142 Pacers are planned to be replaced by the end of 2019 but Classes 144 and 153 (and a small number of 142s) are to be retained into 2020.

| **ScotRail** | Abellio (Netherlands Railways) (until 31 March 2022) | **ScotRail** |

There is an option to extend the franchise by 3 years to March 2025.

ScotRail provides almost all passenger services within Scotland and also trains from Glasgow to Carlisle via Dumfries, some of which extend to Newcastle-upon-Tyne (jointly operated with

Northern). The company operates a large fleet of DMUs of Classes 156, 158 and 170 and EMU Classes 314, 318, 320, 334, 380 and 385. Two locomotive-hauled Mark 2 sets are also used on Fife Circle commuter trains, hauled by Class 68s hired from DRS. In 2018 the first of a fleet of refurbished HSTs entered service on InterCity services and this has been supplemented by a number of unrefurbished HSTs which are used between Edinburgh/Glasgow and Aberdeen and Inverness and also Inverness–Aberdeen. All HSTs should be refurbished by the end of 2020.

| **South Eastern** | Govia (Go-Ahead/Keolis) (until 1 April 2020) | **Southeastern** |

The franchise competition was scrapped in 2019. It will either be restarted (in which case another extension to Govia will be required) or the DfT will take over as "Operator of Last Resort" from 2020.

Southeastern operates all services in the south-east London suburbs, the whole of Kent and part of Sussex, which are primarily commuter services to London. It also operates domestic High Speed trains on HS1 from London St Pancras to Ashford, Ramsgate, Dover and Faversham with additional peak services on other routes. EMUs of Classes 375, 376, 377, 465 and 466 are used, along with Class 395s on the High Speed trains.

| **South Western** | First Group (70%)/MTR (30%) (until 17 August 2024) | **South Western Railway** |

There is an option to extend the franchise by 11 months to July 2025.

South Western Railway operates trains from London Waterloo to destinations across the South and South-West including Woking, Basingstoke, Southampton, Portsmouth, Salisbury, Exeter, Reading and Weymouth, as well as suburban services from Waterloo. SWR also runs services between Ryde and Shanklin on the Isle of Wight, using former London Underground 1938 stock (Class 483s). The rest of the fleet consists of DMU Classes 158 and 159 and EMU Classes 442, 444, 450, 455, 456, 458 and 707. A new fleet of Bombardier Class 701s are under construction to replace Classes 455, 456, 458 and 707 from 2020 with a fleet of five third rail Vivarail units (converted former LU D78 stock) on order to replace the 1938 stock on the Isle of Wight.

| **Thameslink, Southern & Great Northern (TSGN)** | Govia (Go-Ahead/Keolis) (until 18 September 2021) | **Govia Thameslink Railway** |

There is an option to extend the franchise by 2 years to September 2023.

Govia operates this franchise, the largest in Great Britain, as a management contract. The former Southern franchise was combined with Thameslink/Great Northern in 2015. GTR uses four brands within the franchise: "Thameslink" for trains between Cambridge North, Peterborough, Bedford and Rainham, Sevenoaks, East Grinstead, Brighton, Littlehampton and Horsham via central London and also on the Sutton/Wimbledon loop using new Class 700 EMUs. "Great Northern" comprises services from London King's Cross and Moorgate to Welwyn Garden City, Hertford North, Peterborough, Cambridge and King's Lynn using Class 365, 387 and 717 EMUs (the final GN Class 313s had been taken out of service as this book closed for press). "Southern" operates predominantly commuter services between London, Surrey and Sussex and "metro" services in South London, as well as services along the south Coast between Southampton, Brighton, Hastings and Ashford, plus the cross-London service from South Croydon to Milton Keynes. Class 171 DMUs are used on Ashford–Eastbourne and London Bridge–Uckfield services, whilst all other services are in the hands of Class 313, 377, 455 and 700 EMUs. Finally, the premium "Gatwick Express" operates non-stop trains between London Victoria, Gatwick Airport and Brighton using Class 387/2 EMUs.

Trans-Pennine Express	First Group	**TransPennine Express**
	(until 31 March 2023)	

There is an option to extend the franchise by 2 years to March 2025.

TransPennine Express operates predominantly long distance inter-urban services linking major cities across the North of England, along with Edinburgh and Glasgow in Scotland. The main services are Manchester Airport/Manchester Piccadilly–Newcastle/Middlesbrough (Redcar from December 2019)/Hull plus Liverpool–Scarborough and Liverpool–Newcastle along the North Trans-Pennine route via Huddersfield, Leeds and York, and Manchester Airport–Cleethorpes along the South Trans-Pennine route via Sheffield. TPE also operates Manchester Airport–Edinburgh/Glasgow (and Liverpool–Glasgow from December 2019). The fleet consists of Class 185 DMUs, plus Class 350 EMUs used on Manchester Airport–Scotland services. Three new fleets are due to be introduced in 2019–20, loco-hauled Class 68+CAF Mark 5A sets (in traffic from August 2019), Class 397 EMUs and Class 802 bi-mode units (in traffic from September 2019).

Wales & Borders	KeolisAmey	**Transport for Wales**
	(until 15 October 2033)	

Franchise procured by the Welsh Government.

Transport for Wales Rail operates a mix of long distance, regional and local services throughout Wales, including the Valley Lines network of lines around Cardiff, and also through services to the English border counties and to Manchester and Birmingham. The fleet consists of DMUs of Classes 142, 143, 150, 153, 158, 170 and 175 and two locomotive-hauled Mark 3 sets: one used on a premium Welsh Government sponsored service on the Cardiff–Holyhead route, and one used between Manchester/Crewe and Holyhead (both are hauled by a Class 67). Rebuilt Class 230 D-Trains are to be introduced on a number of routes from late 2019 and new Stadler and CAF fleets introduced on other routes from 2021.

West Coast Partnership	Virgin Rail Group (Virgin/Stagecoach Group)	**Virgin Trains**
	(until 7 December 2019)	

In August 2019 a consortium of First Group and Trenitalia won the new West Coast franchise, which will run until March 2031 and also include the first years of the planned HS2 services.

Virgin Trains operates long distance services along the West Coast Main Line from London Euston to Birmingham/Wolverhampton, Manchester, Liverpool, Blackpool North and Glasgow using Class 390 Pendolino EMUs. It also operates Class 221 Voyagers on the Euston–Chester–Holyhead route and a small number of trains from Wolverhampton to Shrewsbury, whilst a mixture of Class 221s and 390s are used on the Euston–Birmingham–Glasgow/Edinburgh route.

West Midlands Trains	Abellio (70%)/JR East (15%)/Mitsui (15%)	**West Midlands Railway/**
	(until 31 March 2026)	**London Northwestern**

There is an option to extend the franchise by 2 years to March 2028.

West Midlands Trains operates services under two brand names. West Midlands Railway trains are local and regional services around Birmingham, including to Stratford-upon-Avon, Worcester, Hereford, Redditch, Rugeley and Shrewsbury. WMR is managed by a consortium of 16 councils and the Department for Transport. London Northwestern is the brand used for long distance and regional services from London Euston to Northampton and Birmingham/Crewe and also between Birmingham and Liverpool, Bedford–Bletchley and Watford Junction–St Albans Abbey. The fleet consists of DMU Classes 139, 150, 153, 170 and 172 and EMU Classes 319, 323 and 350. Class 230 D-Trains were introduced onto the Bedford–Bletchley route in 2019 and new DMUs and EMUs will also be introduced on a number of routes in 2020–21.

NON-FRANCHISED SERVICES

The following operators run non-franchised, or "open access" services (* special seasonal services):

Operator	Trading Name	Route
Heathrow Airport Holdings	Heathrow Express	London Paddington–Heathrow Airport

Heathrow Express operates a frequent express passenger service between London Paddington and Heathrow Airport using Class 332 EMUs, now operated by Great Western Railway as part of its franchise.

Hull Trains (part of First)	Hull Trains	London King's Cross–Hull

Hull Trains operates seven trains a day (weekdays) from Hull to London King's Cross via the East Coast Main Line using Class 180 DMUs. One train in each direction starts back from and extends to Beverley. New Class 802s are to be introduced in late 2019.

Grand Central (part of Arriva)	Grand Central	London King's Cross–Sunderland/ Bradford Interchange

Grand Central operates five trains a day from Sunderland and four trains a day from Bradford Interchange to London King's Cross using Class 180 DMUs.

Locomotive Services (TOC)	Locomotive Services	

Locomotive Services operates various excursions across the network.

North Yorkshire Moors Railway Enterprises	North Yorkshire Moors Railway	Pickering–Grosmont–Whitby/ Battersby, Sheringham–Cromer*

The North Yorkshire Moors Railway operates services on the national network between Grosmont and Whitby or Grosmont and Battersby as an extension of its Pickering–Grosmont services and also operates services between Sheringham and Cromer on behalf of the North Norfolk Railway.

South Yorkshire Supertram	Stagecoach Supertram	Meadowhall South–Rotherham Parkgate

South Yorkshire Supertram holds a passenger licence to allow the operation of the pilot tram-train service linking Sheffield city centre with Rotherham Central and Rotherham Parkgate.

Tyne & Wear PTE	Tyne & Wear Metro	Pelaw–Sunderland

Tyne & Wear Passenger Transport Executive holds a passenger license to allow the operation of its Metro service over Network Rail tracks between Pelaw and Sunderland.

| Vintage Trains | Vintage Trains | Birmingham Snow Hill–Stratford-upon-Avon* |

Vintage Trains operates steam-hauled services on a seasonal basis.

| West Coast Railway Company | West Coast Railway Company | Fort William–Mallaig* York–Settle–Carlisle* Carnforth–York–Scarborough* |

WCRC operates steam-hauled services on these routes on a seasonal basis and other excursions across the network.

INTERNATIONAL PASSENGER OPERATORS

Eurostar International operates passenger services between London St Pancras and mainland Europe. The company, established in 2010, is jointly owned by SNCF (the national operator of France): 55%, SNCB (the national operator of Belgium): 5% and Patina Rail: 40%. Patina Rail is made up of Canadian-based Caisse de dépôt et placement du Québec (CDPG) and UK-based Hermes Infrastructure (owning 30% and 10% respectively). This 40% was previously owned by the UK Government until it was sold in 2015.

In addition, a service for the conveyance of accompanied road vehicles through the Channel Tunnel is provided by the tunnel operating company, Eurotunnel. All Eurotunnel services are operated in top-and-tail mode by the powerful Class 9 Bo-Bo-Bo locomotives.

FREIGHT TRAIN OPERATORS

The following operators operate freight services or empty passenger stock workings under "open access" arrangements:

Colas Rail
DB Cargo (UK)
Devon & Cornwall Railways
Direct Rail Services
Freightliner
GB Railfreight
Loram (UK)
Rail Operations Group
West Coast Railway Company

In addition, Amey, Balfour Beatty Rail, Harsco Rail, Loram (UK), South Western Railway, Swietelsky Babcock Rail (SB Rail) and VolkerRail operate trains formed of On-Track Machines.

INTRODUCTION

This book contains details of all locomotive-hauled or propelled coaching stock, often referred to as carriages, which can run on Britain's national railway network.

The number of locomotive-hauled or propelled carriages in use on the national railway network is much fewer than was once the case. Those that remain fall into two distinct groups.

Firstly, there are those used by franchised and open access operators for regular timetabled services. Most of these are formed in fixed or semi-fixed formations with either locomotives or a locomotive and Driving Brake Carriage at either end which allows for push-pull operation. There are also a small number of mainly overnight and peak-hour trains with variable formations that use conventional locomotive haulage.

Secondly there are those used for what can best be described as excursion trains. These include a wide range of carriage types ranging from luxurious saloons to those more suited to the "bucket and spade" seaside type of excursion. These are formed into sets to suit the requirements of the day. From time to time some see limited use with franchised and open access operators to cover for stock shortages and times of exceptional demand such as major sporting events.

In addition, there remain a small number of carriages referred to as "Service Stock" which are used internally within the railway industry and are not used to convey passengers.

FRANCHISED & OPEN ACCESS OPERATORS

For each operator regularly using locomotive-hauled carriages brief details are given here of the sphere of operation. For details of operators using HSTs see Section 2.

Caledonian Sleeper
This franchise, operated by Serco, started in 2015 when the Anglo-Scottish Sleeper operation was split from the ScotRail franchise. Caledonian Sleeper comprises seating and sleeping car services between London Euston and Scotland using sets of Mark 3 Sleeping Cars and Mark 2 seating and catering carriages. These are currently being replaced by a new fleet of CAF Mark 5 carriages with the replacement due to be completed in October 2019.

GBRf is contracted to supply the motive power for the Sleepers. Class 92s are used between London Euston and Edinburgh/Glasgow Central and rebuilt Class 73/9s between Edinburgh and Inverness, Aberdeen and Fort William.

Chiltern Railways
Chiltern operates four sets of Mark 3 carriages with DRS Class 68 locomotives on its Mainline services between London Marylebone and Birmingham Moor Street/Kidderminster (plus one train to Oxford). Another

set is used on a peak-hour commuter service between Marylebone and Bicester North or Banbury. All trains operate as push-pull sets.

Greater Anglia
The Inter-City service between London Liverpool Street and Norwich is operated using 12 sets of Mark 3 carriages with Class 90 locomotives in push-pull formations. These are due to be replaced by new Class 745 EMUs by early 2020.

Great Western Railway
The "Night Riviera" seating and sleeping car service between London Paddington and Penzance uses sets of Mark 3 carriages hauled by Class 57/6 locomotives.

London North Eastern Railway
LNER operates sets of Mark 4 carriages with Class 91 locomotives in push-pull formations on its Inter-City services between London King's Cross and Yorkshire, North-East England and Scotland. These are currently being replaced by new Class 800/801 "Azuma" units.

North Yorkshire Moors Railway
In addition to operating the North Yorkshire Moors Railway between Pickering and Grosmont the company operates through services to Whitby and occasionally Battersby. A fleet of Mark 1 passenger carriages and Pullman Cars are used for these services. It also operates the "North Norfolkman" services on behalf of the North Norfolk Railway between Sheringham and Cromer.

ScotRail
ScotRail operates two sets of Mark 2 carriages supplied by DRS on peak-hour services between Edinburgh and Fife using Class 68s.

Transport for Wales
The Monday–Friday Welsh Government sponsored train between Cardiff and Holyhead uses Mark 3 carriages in push-pull mode with a Class 67. A second similarly formed set is used for weekday trains between Crewe or Manchester and Chester/North Wales. These carriages are also used for relief trains, particularly in connection with sports fixtures at Cardiff and busy ferry sailings to and from Holyhead. The Mark 3s are due to be replaced by Mark 4s during 2020.

West Coast Railway Company
WCRC operates two sets of Mark 1/2 carriages on its steam-hauled "Jacobite" trains between Fort William and Mallaig. These trains normally operate between late April and late October.

EXCURSION TRAIN OPERATORS

Usually, three types of companies will be involved in the operation of an excursion train. There will be the promoter, the rolling stock provider and the train operator. In many cases two or more of these roles may be undertaken by the same or associated companies. Only a small number of Train Operating Companies facilitate the operation of excursion trains. This takes various forms ranging from the complete package of providing and operating the train, through offering a "hook up and haul" service, to operating the train for a third party rolling stock custodian.

DB Cargo UK
DBC currently operates its own luxurious train of Mark 3 carriages, called the Company Train. It also offers a hook up and haul service and regularly operates the Royal Train and the Belmond British Pullman as well as trains for Riviera Trains and Locomotives Services and their client promoters.

Direct Rail Services
DRS operates a fleet of Mark 2 carriages originally intended for use on excursion trains. These are currently hired to ScotRail for use on regular timetabled services. The company also offers a hook up and haul service for Riviera Trains and its client promoters.

GB Railfreight
GBRf initially operated excursion trains using the preserved Class 201 "Hastings" DEMU. It now also operates a small number of company excursions using hired carriages. The company also offers a hook up and haul service operating the Royal Scotsman luxury train, as well as trains for Riviera Trains and its client promoters.

Locomotive Services
This vertically integrated company gained a license in 2017. From its base at Crewe excursion trains are operated using its fleet of steam and diesel locomotives and Mark 1/2 carriages.

Rail Operations Group
This company operates a small number of excursion trains using hired in carriages. It also offers a hook up and haul service.

Vintage Trains
This vertically integrated company gained a licence in September 2018. From its base at Tyseley it operates the "Shakespeare Express" steam service between Birmingham and Stratford-upon-Avon. It also operates excursions using its fleet of steam and diesel locomotives and Mark 1/2 carriages and Pullman cars.

West Coast Railway Company
This vertically integrated company has its own fleet of steam and diesel locomotives as well as a full range of different carriage types. It operates its own regular trains, including the luxury Northern Belle, the "Jacobite" steam service between Fort William and Mallaig, the "Dalesman" steam and diesel services over the Settle & Carlisle route and numerous excursion trains for itself and client promoters. In addition, it offers a hook up and haul service operating trains for The Princess Royal Locomotive Trust, Locomotives Services and the Scottish Railway Preservation Society.

LAYOUT OF INFORMATION

Carriages are listed in numerical order of painted number in batches according to type.

Where a carriage has been renumbered, the former number is shown in parentheses. If a carriage has been renumbered more than once, the original number is shown first in parentheses, followed by the most recent previous number.

Each carriage entry is laid out as in the following example (previous number(s) column may be omitted where not applicable):

No.	Prev. No.	Notes	Livery	Owner	Operator	Depot/Location
82301	(82117)	g	**CM**	AV	CR	AL

Codes: Codes are used to denote the livery, owner, operator and depot/location of each carriage. Details of codes used can be found in Section 10 of this book.

The owner is the responsible custodian of the carriage and this may not always be the legal owner. Actual ownership can be very complicated. Some vehicles are owned by finance/leasing companies. Others are owned by subsidiary companies of a holding company or by an associate company of the responsible custodian or operator.

The operator is the organisation which facilitates the use of the carriage and may not be the actual train operating company which runs the train. If no operator is shown the carriage is considered to be not in use.

The depot is the facility primarily responsible for the carriages maintenance. Light maintenance and heavy overhauls may be carried out elsewhere.

The location is where carriages not in use are currently being kept or stored.

GENERAL INFORMATION

CLASSIFICATION AND NUMBERING

Seven different numbering systems were in use on British Rail. These were the British Rail series, the four pre-nationalisation companies' series', the Pullman Car Company's series and the UIC (International Union of Railways) series. In this book BR number series carriages and former Pullman Car Company series are listed separately. There is also a separate listing of "Saloon" type carriages, that includes pre-nationalisation survivors, which are permitted to run on the national railway system, Locomotive Support Carriages and Service Stock. Please note the Mark 2 Pullman carriages were ordered after the Pullman Car Company had been nationalised and are therefore numbered in the British Rail series. The new CAF Mark 5 carriages currently being delivered have been allocated numbers in the British Rail series.

Also listed separately are the British Rail and Pullman Car Company number series carriages used on North Yorkshire Moors Railway and North Norfolk Railway services on the national railway network. This is due to their very restricted sphere of operation.

The BR number series grouped carriages of a particular type together in chronological order. Major modifications affecting type of accommodation resulted in renumbering into a more appropriate or new number series. Since privatisation such renumbering has not always taken place resulting in renumbering which has been more haphazard and greater variations within numbering groups.

With the introduction of the TOPS numbering system, coaching stock (including multiple unit vehicles) retained their original BR number unless this conflicted with a locomotive number. Carriages can be one–five digits, although no one or two-digit examples remain in use on the national network. BR generally numbered "Service Stock" in a six-digit wagon number series.

UNITS OF MEASUREMENT

All dimensions and weights are quoted for carriages in an "as new" condition or after a major modification, such as fitting with new bogies etc. Dimensions are quoted in the order length x width. Lengths quoted are over buffers or couplers as appropriate. All widths quoted are maxima. All weights are shown as metric tonnes (t = tonnes).

DIMENSIONS

Carriage lengths are summarised as follows:

Mark 1: 19.35 m or 17.37 m.   **Mark 4**: 23.00 m.
Mark 2: 19.66 m.   **Mark 5**: 22.20 m.
Mark 3: 23.00 m.   **Mark 5A**: 22.20–22.37 m.
Mark 3 HST: 23.00 m.

DETAILED INFORMATION & CODES

Under each type heading, the following details are shown:

- "Mark" of carriage (see below).
- Descriptive text.
- Number of First Class seats, Standard Class seats, lavatory compartments and wheelchair spaces shown as F/S nT nW respectively. A number in brackets indicates tip-up seats (in addition to the regular seats).
- Bogie type (see below).
- Additional features.
- ETS Index.
- Weight: All weights are shown as metric tonnes.

BOGIE TYPES

Gresley. LNER design of bogie first used in the "Gresley" era. Used by BR on some Mark 1 catering carriages. Now used for some saloons.

BR Mark 1 (BR1). Double bolster leaf spring bogie. Generally 90 mph, but Mark 1 bogies may be permitted to run at 100 mph with special maintenance. Weight: 6.1 t.

BR Mark 2 (BR2). Single bolster leaf-spring bogie used on certain types of non-passenger stock and suburban stock (all now withdrawn). Weight: 5.3 t.

COMMONWEALTH (C). Heavy, cast steel coil spring bogie. 100 mph. Weight: 6.75 t.

B4. Coil spring fabricated bogie. Generally 100 mph, but B4 bogies may be permitted to run at 110 mph with special maintenance. Weight: 5.2 t.

B5. Heavy duty version of B4. 100 mph. Weight: 5.3 t.

B5 (SR). A bogie originally used on Southern Region EMUs, similar in design to B5. Now also used on locomotive-hauled carriages. 100 mph.

BT10. A fabricated bogie designed for 125 mph. Air suspension.

T4. A 125 mph bogie designed by BREL (now Bombardier Transportation).

BT41. Fitted to Mark 4 carriages, designed by SIG in Switzerland. At present limited to 125 mph, but designed for 140 mph.

CAF. Fitted to CAF Mark 5 and Mark 5A carriages.

BRAKES

Air braking is now standard on British main line trains. Carriages with other equipment are denoted:

b   Air braked, through vacuum pipe.
v   Vacuum braked.
x   Dual braked (air and vacuum).

HEATING & VENTILATION

Electric heating and ventilation is now standard on British main-line trains. Certain carriages for use on excursion services may also have steam heating facilities, or be steam heated only. All carriages used on North Yorkshire Moors Railway and North Norfolk Railway trains have steam heating.

NOTES ON ELECTRIC TRAIN SUPPLY

The sum of ETS indices in a train must not be more than the ETS index of the locomotive or generator van. The normal voltage on British trains is 1000 V. Suffix "X" denotes 600 amp wiring instead of 400 amp. Trains whose ETS index is higher than 66 must be formed completely of 600 amp wired stock. Class 33 and 73/1 locomotives cannot provide a suitable electric train supply for Mark 2D, Mark 2E, Mark 2F, Mark 3, Mark 3A, Mark 3B or Mark 4 carriages. Class 55 locomotives provide an ETS directly from one of their traction generators into the train line. Consequently voltage fluctuations can result in motor-alternator flashover. Thus these locomotives are not suitable for use with Mark 2D, Mark 2E, Mark 2F, Mark 3, Mark 3A, Mark 3B or Mark 4 carriages unless modified motor-alternators are fitted. Such motor alternators were fitted to Mark 2D and 2F carriages used on the East Coast Main Line, but few remain fitted.

PUBLIC ADDRESS

It is assumed all carriages are now fitted with public address equipment, although certain stored carriages may not have this feature. In addition, it is assumed all carriages with a conductor's compartment have public address transmission facilities, as have catering carriages.

COOKING EQUIPMENT

It is assumed that Mark 1 catering carriages have gas powered cooking equipment, whilst Mark 2, 3 and 4 catering carriages have electric powered cooking equipment unless stated otherwise.

ADDITIONAL FEATURE CODES

d	Central Door Locking.
dg	Driver–Guard communication equipment.
f	Facelifted or fluorescent lighting.
h	"High density" seating
k	Composition brake blocks (instead of cast iron).
n	Day/night lighting.
pg	Public address transmission and driver-guard communication.
pt	Public address transmission facility.
q	Catering staff to shore telephone.
w	Wheelchair space.

BUILD DETAILS

Lot Numbers
Vehicles ordered under the auspices of BR were allocated a lot (batch) number when ordered and these are quoted in class headings and sub-headings.

Builders
These are shown in class headings, the following designations being used:

Ashford	BR, Ashford Works.
BRCW	Birmingham Railway Carriage & Wagon Company, Smethwick, Birmingham.
BREL Derby	BREL, Derby Carriage Works (later ABB/Adtranz Derby, now Bombardier Transportation Derby).
Charles Roberts	Charles Roberts & Company, Horbury, Wakefield (later Bombardier Transportation).
Cravens	Cravens, Sheffield.
Derby	BR, Derby Carriage Works (later BREL Derby, then ABB/Adtranz Derby, now Bombardier Transportation Derby).
Doncaster	BR, Doncaster Works (later BREL Doncaster, then BRML Doncaster, then ABB/Adtranz Doncaster, then Bombardier).
Eastleigh	BR, Eastleigh Works (later BREL Eastleigh, then Wessex Traincare, and Alstom Eastleigh, now Arlington Fleet Services).
Glasgow	BR Springburn Works, Glasgow (now Knorr-Bremse Rail Systems).
Gloucester	The Gloucester Railway Carriage & Wagon Co.
Hunslet-Barclay	Hunslet Barclay, Kilmarnock Works (now Wabtec Rail Scotland).
Metro-Cammell	Metropolitan-Cammell, Saltley, Birmingham (later GEC-Alsthom Birmingham, then Alstom Birmingham).
Pressed Steel	Pressed Steel, Linwood.
Swindon	BR Swindon Works.
Wolverton	BR Wolverton Works (later BREL Wolverton then Railcare, Wolverton, then Alstom, Wolverton now Knorr-Bremse Rail Systems).
York	BR, York Carriage Works (later BREL York, then ABB York).

Information on sub-contracting works which built parts of vehicles eg the underframes etc is not shown. In addition to the above, certain vintage Pullman cars were built or rebuilt at the following works:

Metropolitan Carriage & Wagon Company, Birmingham (later Alstom).
Midland Carriage & Wagon Company, Birmingham.
Pullman Car Company, Preston Park, Brighton.
Conversions have also been carried out at the Railway Technical Centre, Derby, LNWR, Crewe and Blakes Fabrications, Edinburgh.

ABBREVIATIONS

The following abbreviations are used in class headings and also throughout
this publication:

BR	British Railways.
DB	Deutsche Bahn
DEMU	Diesel Electric Multiple Unit.
DMU	Diesel Multiple Unit (general term).
EMU	Electric Multiple Unit.
ETH	Electric Train Heating
ft	feet
GWR	Great Western Railway
kN	kilonewtons.
km/h	kilometres per hour.
kW	kilowatts.
LT	London Transport.
LUL	London Underground Limited.
m	metres.
mph	miles per hour.
SR	BR Southern Region

1. BRITISH RAILWAYS NUMBER SERIES COACHING STOCK

KITCHEN FIRST

Mark 1. Spent most of its life as a Royal Train vehicle and was numbered 2907 for a time. 24/–. B5 bogies. ETS 2.

Lot No. 30633 Swindon 1961. 41 t.

325	**VN**	WC	*WC*	CS	DUART

PULLMAN KITCHEN

Mark 2. Pressure Ventilated. Built with First Class seating but this has been replaced with a servery area. Gas cooking. 2T. B5 bogies. ETS 6.

Lot No. 30755 Derby 1966. 40 t.

504	**PC**	WC	*WC*	CS	ULLSWATER
506	**PC**	WC	*WC*	CS	WINDERMERE

PULLMAN OPEN FIRST

Mark 2. Pressure Ventilated. 36/– 2T. B4 bogies. ETS 5.

Lot No. 30754 Derby 1966. 35 t.

Non-standard livery: 546 Maroon & beige.

546	**0**	WC		CS	CITY OF MANCHESTER
548	**PC**	WC	*WC*	CS	GRASMERE
549	**PC**	WC	*WC*	CS	BASSENTHWAITE
550	**PC**	WC	*WC*	CS	RYDAL WATER
551	**PC**	WC	*WC*	CS	BUTTERMERE
552	**PC**	WC	*WC*	CS	ENNERDALE WATER
553	**PC**	WC	*WC*	CS	CRUMMOCK WATER

PULLMAN OPEN BRAKE FIRST

Mark 2. Pressure Ventilated. 30/– 2T. B4 bogies. ETS 4.

Lot No. 30753 Derby 1966. 35 t.

586	**PC**	WC	*WC*	CS	DERWENTWATER

BUFFET FIRST

Mark 2F. Air conditioned. Converted 1988–89/91 at BREL, Derby from Mark 2F Open Firsts. 1200/03/11/20/21 have Stones equipment, others have Temperature Ltd. 25/– 1T 1W. B4 bogies. d. ETS 6X.

1200/03/11/20. Lot No. 30845 Derby 1973. 33 t.
1207/10/12/21. Lot No. 30859 Derby 1973–74. 33 t.

1200	(3287, 6459)	**BG**	RV	*RV*	BU
1203	(3291)	**CC**	LS	*LS*	CL
1207	(3328, 6422)	**V**	WC		CS
1210	(3405, 6462)	**FS**	CA	*CA*	PO
1211	(3305)	**PC**	LS	*LS*	CL	SNAEFELL
1212	(3427, 6453)	**BG**	RV	*RV*	BU
1220	(3315, 6432)	**FS**	CA	*CA*	PO
1221	(3371)	**IC**	WC		CS

KITCHEN WITH BAR

Mark 1. Built with no seats but three Pullman-style seats now fitted in bar area. B5 bogies. ETS 1.

Lot No. 30624 Cravens 1960–61. 41 t.

1566		**VN**	WC	*WC*	CS	CAERDYDD

KITCHEN BUFFET UNCLASSIFIED

Mark 1. Built with 23 loose chairs. All remaining vehicles were refurbished with 23 fixed polypropylene chairs and fluorescent lighting. 1683/91 were further refurbished with 21 chairs, wheelchair space and carpets. ETS 2 (* 2X).

Now used on excursion trains with the seating area adapted to various uses including servery and food preparation areas, with some or all seating removed.

1651–91. Lot No. 30628 Pressed Steel 1960–61. Commonwealth bogies. 39 t.
1730. Lot No. 30512 BRCW 1960–61. B5 bogies. 37 t.

1651		**CC**	RV	*RV*	ZG		1683		**RB**	RV		BU
1657		**BG**	RV	*RV*	BU		1691		**BG**	RV	*RV*	BU
1666	x	**M**	RP	*WC*	CS		1730	x	**M**	SP	*SP*	BO
1671	x*	**CH**	RV	*RV*	ZG							

BUFFET STANDARD

Mark 1. These carriages are basically an open standard with two full window spaces removed to accommodate a buffet counter, and four seats removed to allow for a stock cupboard. All remaining vehicles now have fluorescent lighting. –/44 2T. Commonwealth bogies. ETS 3.

1861 has had its toilets replaced with store cupboards.

1813–32. Lot No. 30520 Wolverton 1960. 38 t.
1840. Lot No. 30507 Wolverton 1960. 37 t.
1859–63. Lot No. 30670 Wolverton 1961–62. 38 t.
1882. Lot No. 30702 Wolverton 1962. 38 t.

1813	x	**CH**	RV	*RV*	ZG	1860	x	**M**	WC	*WC*	CS
1832	x	**CH**	RV	*RV*	ZG	1861	x	**M**	WC	*WC*	CS
1840	v	**M**	WC	*WC*	CS	1863	x	**CH**	LS		CL
1859	x	**M**	SP	*SP*	BO	1882	x	**M**	WC	*WC*	CS

KITCHEN UNCLASSIFIED

Mark 1. These carriages were built as Unclassified Restaurants. They were rebuilt with buffet counters and 23 fixed polypropylene chairs, then further refurbished by fitting fluorescent lighting. Further modified for use as servery vehicle with seating removed and kitchen extended. ETS 2X.

1953. Lot No. 30575 Swindon 1960. B4/B5 bogies. 36.5 t.
1961. Lot No. 30632 Swindon 1961. Commonwealth bogies. 39 t.

1953		**VN**	WC	*WC*	CS	1961	x	**M**	WC	*WC*	CS

HM THE QUEEN'S SALOON

Mark 3. Converted from an Open First built 1972. Consists of a lounge, bedroom and bathroom for HM The Queen, and a combined bedroom and bathroom for the Queen's dresser. One entrance vestibule has double doors. Air conditioned. BT10 bogies. ETS 9X.

Lot No. 30886 Wolverton 1977. 36 t.

2903	(11001)	**RP**	NR	*RT*	ZN

HRH THE DUKE OF EDINBURGH'S SALOON

Mark 3. Converted from an Open Standard built 1972. Consists of a combined lounge/dining room, a bedroom and a shower room for the Duke, a kitchen and a valet's bedroom and bathroom. Air conditioned. BT10 bogies. ETS 15X.

Lot No. 30887 Wolverton 1977. 36 t.

2904	(12001)	**RP**	NR	*RT*	ZN

ROYAL HOUSEHOLD SLEEPING CAR

Mark 3A. Built to similar specification as Sleeping Cars 10647–729. 12 sleeping compartments for use of Royal Household with a fixed lower berth and a hinged upper berth. 2T plus shower room. Air conditioned. BT10 bogies. ETS 11X.

Lot No. 31002 Derby/Wolverton 1985. 44 t.

2915   **RP**   NR   *RT*   ZN

HRH THE PRINCE OF WALES'S DINING CAR

Mark 3. Converted from HST TRUK (kitchen car) built 1976. Large kitchen retained, but dining area modified for Royal use seating up to 14 at central table(s). Air conditioned. BT10 bogies. ETS 13X.

Lot No. 31059 Wolverton 1988. 43 t.

2916   (40512)   **RP**   NR   *RT*   ZN

ROYAL KITCHEN/HOUSEHOLD DINING CAR

Mark 3. Converted from HST TRUK built 1977. Large kitchen retained and dining area slightly modified with seating for 22 Royal Household members. Air conditioned. BT10 bogies. ETS 13X.

Lot No. 31084 Wolverton 1990. 43 t.

2917   (40514)   **RP**   NR   *RT*   ZN

ROYAL HOUSEHOLD CARS

Mark 3. Converted from HST TRUKs built 1976/77. Air conditioned. BT10 bogies. ETS 10X.

Lot Nos. 31083 (* 31085) Wolverton 1989. 41.05 t.

2918   (40515)   **RP**   NR   ZN
2919   (40518) *   **RP**   NR   ZN

ROYAL HOUSEHOLD COUCHETTES

Mark 2B. Converted from Corridor Brake First built 1969. Consists of luggage accommodation, guard's compartment, workshop area, 350 kW diesel generator and staff sleeping accommodation. B5 bogies. ETS 2X (when generator not in use). ETS index ?? (when generator in use).

Lot No. 31044 Wolverton 1986. 48 t.

2920   (14109, 17109)   **RP**   NR   *RT*   ZN

Mark 2B. Converted from Corridor Brake First built 1969. Consists of luggage accommodation, kitchen, brake control equipment and staff accommodation. B5 bogies. ETS 7X.

Lot No. 31086 Wolverton 1990. 41.5 t.

2921   (14107, 17107)   **RP**   NR   *RT*   ZN

HRH THE PRINCE OF WALES'S SLEEPING CAR

Mark 3B. Air conditioned. BT10 bogies. ETS 7X.

Lot No. 31035 Derby/Wolverton 1987.

2922   **RP**   NR   *RT*   ZN

ROYAL SALOON

Mark 3B. Air conditioned. BT10 bogies. ETS 6X.

Lot No. 31036 Derby/Wolverton 1987.

2923   **RP**   NR   *RT*   ZN

OPEN FIRST

Mark 1. 42/– 2T. ETS 3. Many now fitted with table lamps.

3058 was numbered DB 975313, 3068 was numbered DB 975606 and 3093 was numbered DB 977594 for a time when in departmental service for BR.

3058–68. Lot No. 30169 Doncaster 1955. B4 bogies. 33 t (* Commonwealth bogies 35 t).
3093. Lot No. 30472 BRCW 1959. B4 bogies. 33 t.
3096–3100. Lot No. 30576 BRCW 1959. B4 bogies. 33 t.

3058	*x **M**	WC	*WC*	CS	FLORENCE	3096	x **M**	SP *SP*	BO
3066	**CC**	RV	*RV*	ZG		3097	**CH**	RV *RV*	ZG
3068	**CC**	RV	*RV*	ZG		3098	x **CH**	RV *RV*	ZG
3093	x **M**	WC	*WC*	CS	FLORENCE	3100	x **CC**	LS *LS*	CL

Later design with fluorescent lighting, aluminium window frames and Commonwealth bogies.

3128/36/41/43/46/47/48 were renumbered 1058/60/63/65/68/69/70 when reclassified Restaurant Open First, then 3600/05/08/09/06/04/10 when declassified to Open Standard, but have since regained their original numbers. 3136 was numbered DB 977970 for a time when in use with Serco Railtest as a Brake Force Runner.

3105 has had its luggage racks removed and has tungsten lighting.

3105–28. Lot No. 30697 Swindon 1962–63. 36 t.
3130–50. Lot No. 30717 Swindon 1963. 36 t.

3105	x	**M**	WC	*WC*	CS		3125	x	**CC**	LS	*LS*	CL
3106	x	**M**	WC	*WC*	CS		3128	x	**M**	WC	*WC*	CS
3110	x	**CH**	RV	*RV*	ZG		3130	x	**M**	WC	*WC*	CS
3112	x	**CH**	RV		ZG		3136	x	**M**	WC	*WC*	CS
3113	x	**M**	WC	*WC*	CS		3141		**CH**	RV	*RV*	ZG
3115	x	**M**	SP	*SP*	BO		3143	x	**M**	WC	*WC*	CS
3117	x	**M**	WC	*WC*	CS		3146		**CH**	RV	*RV*	ZG
3119	x	**CH**	RV	*RV*	ZG		3147		**CH**	RV	*RV*	ZG
3120		**CH**	RV	*RV*	ZG		3148		**CC**	LS		CL
3121		**CH**	RV	*RV*	ZG		3149		**CH**	RV	*RV*	ZG
3122	x	**CC**	LS	*LS*	CL		3150		**M**	SP	*SP*	BO
3123		**CH**	RV	*RV*	ZG							

Names:

3105	JULIA		3128	VICTORIA
3106	ALEXANDRA		3130	PAMELA
3113	JESSICA		3136	DIANA
3117	CHRISTINA		3143	PATRICIA

OPEN FIRST

Mark 2D. Air conditioned. Stones equipment. 42/– 2T. B4 bogies. ETS 5.

† Interior modified to Pullman Car standards with new seating, new panelling, tungsten lighting and table lights.

Lot No. 30821 Derby 1971–72. 34 t.

3174	†	**VN**	WC	*WC*	CS	GLAMIS
3182	†	**VN**	WC	*WC*	CS	WARWICK
3188		**PC**	LS		CL	CADAIR IDRIS

OPEN FIRST

Mark 2E. Air conditioned. Stones equipment. 42/– 2T (* 36/– 2T). B4 bogies. ETS 5.

r Refurbished with new seats.
† Interior modified to Pullman Car standards with new seating, new panelling, tungsten lighting and table lights.

Lot No. 30843 Derby 1972–73. 32.5 t. († 35.8 t).

3223		**RV**	LS		CL	DIAMOND
3229		**PC**	LS	*LS*	CL	SNOWDON
3231	*	**PC**	LS	*LS*	CL	BEN CRUACHAN
3232	dr	**BG**	WC		CS	
3240		**RV**	LS		CL	SAPPHIRE
3247	†	**VN**	WC	*WC*	CS	CHATSWORTH
3267	†	**VN**	WC	*WC*	CS	BELVOIR
3273	†	**VN**	WC	*WC*	CS	ALNWICK
3275	†	**VN**	WC	*WC*	CS	HARLECH

OPEN FIRST

Mark 2F. Air conditioned. 3278–3314/3359–79 have Stones equipment, others have Temperature Ltd. All refurbished in the 1980s with power-operated vestibule doors, new panels and new seat trim. 42/– 2T. B4 bogies. d. ETS 5X.

r Further refurbished with table lamps and modified seats with burgundy seat trim.
u Fitted with power supply for Mark 1 Kitchen Buffet Unclassified.

3278–3314. Lot No. 30845 Derby 1973. 33.5 t.
3325–3426. Lot No. 30859 Derby 1973–74. 33.5 t.
3431–3438. Lot No. 30873 Derby 1974–75. 33.5 t.

3278	r	**BG**	RV	*RV*	BU		3356	r	**BG**	RV	*RV*	BU
3304	r	**BG**	RV	*RV*	BU		3359	r	**M**	WC	*WC*	CS
3312		**PC**	LS	*LS*	CL		3360	r	**PC**	WC	*WC*	CS
3313	r	**M**	WC	*WC*	CS		3362	r	**PC**	WC	*WC*	CS
3314	r	**BG**	RV	*RV*	BU		3364	r	**BG**	RV	*RV*	BU
3325	r	**V**	RV		ZG		3384	r	**PC**	LS	*LS*	CL
3326	r	**M**	WC	*WC*	CS		3386	r	**BG**	RV	*RV*	BU
3330	r	**CC**	LS	*LS*	CL		3390	r	**BG**	RV	*RV*	BU
3333	r	**BG**	RV	*RV*	BU		3392	r	**M**	WC	*WC*	CS
3340	r	**BG**	RV	*RV*	BU		3395	r	**M**	WC	*WC*	CS
3344	r	**PC**	LS	*LS*	CL		3397	r	**BG**	RV	*RV*	BU
3345	r	**BG**	RV	*RV*	BU		3426	r	**PC**	LS	*LS*	CL
3348	r	**PC**	LS	*LS*	CL		3431	r	**M**	WC	*WC*	CS
3350	r	**M**	WC	*WC*	CS		3438	r	**PC**	LS	*LS*	CL
3352	r	**M**	WC	*WC*	CS							

Names:

3312	HELVELLYN		3384	PEN-Y-GHENT
3344	SCAFELL		3426	BEN NEVIS
3348	INGLEBOROUGH		3438	BEN LOMOND

OPEN STANDARD

Mark 1. –/64 2T. ETS 4.

4831–36. Lot No. 30506 Wolverton 1959. Commonwealth bogies. 33 t.
4854/56. Lot No. 30525 Wolverton 1959–60. B4 bogies. 33 t.

4831	x	**M**	SP	*SP*	BO		4854	x	**M**	WC	*WC*	CS
4832	x	**M**	SP	*SP*	BO		4856	x	**M**	SP	*SP*	BO
4836	x	**M**	SP	*SP*	BO							

OPEN STANDARD

Mark 1. Commonwealth bogies. –/64 2T. ETS 4.

4905. Lot No. 30646 Wolverton 1961. 36 t.
4927–5044. Lot No. 30690 Wolverton 1961–62. 37 t.

4905	x	**M**	WC	*WC*	CS	4984	x	**M**	WC	*WC*	CS
4927	x	**CC**	RV	*RV*	ZG	4991		**CH**	RV	*RV*	ZG
4931	v	**M**	WC	*WC*	CS	4994	x	**M**	WC	*WC*	CS
4940	x	**M**	WC	*WC*	CS	4998		**CH**	RV	*RV*	ZG
4946	x	**CH**	RV	*RV*	ZG	5009	x	**CH**	RV		BU
4949	x	**CH**	RV	*RV*	ZG	5028	x	**M**	SP	*SP*	BO
4951	x	**M**	WC	*WC*	CS	5032	x	**M**	WC	*WC*	CS
4954	v	**M**	WC	*WC*	CS	5033	x	**M**	WC	*WC*	CS
4959		**CH**	RV	*RV*	ZG	5035	x	**M**	WC	*WC*	CS
4960	x	**M**	WC	*WC*	CS	5044	x	**M**	WC	*WC*	CS
4973	x	**M**	WC	*WC*	CS						

OPEN STANDARD

Mark 2. Pressure ventilated. –/64 2T. B4 bogies. ETS 4.

Lot No. 30751 Derby 1965–67. 32 t.

5157	v	**CH**	VT	*VT*	TM	5200	v	**M**	WC	*WC*	CS
5171	v	**M**	WC	*WC*	CS	5212	v	**CH**	VT	*VT*	TM
5177	v	**CH**	VT	*VT*	TM	5216	v	**M**	WC	*WC*	CS
5191	v	**CH**	VT	*VT*	TM	5222	v	**M**	WC	*WC*	CS
5198	v	**CH**	VT	*VT*	TM						

OPEN STANDARD

Mark 2. Pressure ventilated. –/48 2T. B4 bogies. ETS 4.

Lot No. 30752 Derby 1966. 32 t.

5229		**M**	WC	*WC*	CS	5239		**M**	WC	*WC*	CS
5236	v	**M**	WC	*WC*	CS	5249	v	**M**	WC	*WC*	CS
5237	v	**M**	WC	*WC*	CS						

OPEN STANDARD

Mark 2A. Pressure ventilated. –/64 2T (w –/62 2T). B4 bogies. ETS 4.

f Facelifted vehicles.

5278–92. Lot No. 30776 Derby 1967–68. 32 t.
5366–5419. Lot No. 30787 Derby 1968. 32 t.

5278		**M**	WC	*WC*	CS	5366	f	**CH**	LS		ZG
5292	f	**CC**	RV		BU	5419	w	**M**	WC	*WC*	CS

OPEN STANDARD

Mark 2B. Pressure ventilated. –/62. B4 bogies. ETS 4.

Lot No. 30791 Derby 1969. 32 t.

5487   **M** WC *WC* CS

OPEN STANDARD

Mark 2E. Air conditioned. Stones equipment. Refurbished with new interior panelling. –/64 2T. B4 bogies. d. ETS 5.

s Modified design of seat headrest and centre luggage stack. –/60 2T.

5787. Lot No. 30837 Derby 1972. 33.5 t.
5810. Lot No. 30844 Derby 1972–73. 33.5 t.

5787 s   **DS** DR *DR* KM | 5810   **DS** DR *DR*   KM

OPEN STANDARD

Mark 2F. Air conditioned. Temperature Ltd equipment. InterCity 70 seats. All were refurbished in the 1980s with power-operated vestibule doors, new panels and seat trim. They have subsequently undergone a second refurbishment with carpets and new seat trim. –/64 2T. B4 bogies. d. ETS 5X.

q Fitted with two wheelchair spaces. –/60 2T 2W.
s Fitted with centre luggage stack. –/60 2T.
t Fitted with centre luggage stack and wheelchair space. –/58 2T 1W.
† Retention toilets.

5910–55. Lot No. 30846 Derby 1973. 33 t.
5961–6158. Lot No. 30860 Derby 1973–74. 33 t.
6173–83. Lot No. 30874 Derby 1974–75. 33 t.

No.		flag				No.		flag			
5910	q	**BG**	RV		BU	5991		**CC**	LS	*LS*	CL
5912		**PC**	LS	*LS*	CL	5995	†	**DS**	DR	*SR*	ML
5919	† pt	**DS**	DR	*DR*	KM	5998		**BG**	RV	*TW*	CF
5921		**AR**	RV	*RV*	BU	6000	t	**M**	WC	*WC*	CS
5929		**BG**	RV	*RV*	BU	6001	†	**DS**	DR	*SR*	ML
5937		**DS**	DR	*DR*	KM	6006		**AR**	RV		BU
5945		**SR**	RV	*SR*	ML	6008	† s	**DS**	DR	*SR*	ML
5950		**AR**	RV	*RV*	BU	6012		**M**	WC	*WC*	CS
5952		**SR**	RV	*SR*	ML	6021		**PC**	WC	*WC*	CS
5955		**SR**	RV	*SR*	ML	6022	s	**M**	WC	*WC*	CS
5961	pt	**BG**	RV	*TW*	CF	6024		**BG**	RV	*TW*	CF
5964		**AR**	RV	*RV*	BU	6027	q	**SR**	RV	*SR*	ML
5965	t	**SR**	RV	*SR*	ML	6042		**AR**	RV	*TW*	CF
5971	†	**DS**	DR	*SR*	ML	6046	†	**DS**	DR	*SR*	ML
5976	t	**SR**	RV	*SR*	ML	6051		**BG**	RV	*RV*	BU
5985		**AR**	RV	*RV*	BU	6054		**BG**	RV	*TW*	CF
5987		**SR**	RV	*SR*	ML	6064	†	**DS**	DR	*SR*	ML

6067	pt	**BG**	RV	_TW_	CF		6141	q	**V**	RV		BU
6103		**M**	WC	_WC_	CS		6158		**BG**	RV	_TW_	CF
6115	s	**M**	WC	_WC_	CS		6173	· †	**DS**	DR	_SR_	ML
6117	†	**DS**	DR	_SR_	ML		6176	t	**SR**	RV	_SR_	ML
6122	†	**DS**	DR	_SR_	ML		6177	s	**SR**	RV	_SR_	ML
6137	s pt	**SR**	RV	_SR_	ML		6183	s	**SR**	RV	_SR_	ML

BRAKE GENERATOR VAN

Mark 1. Renumbered 1989 from BR departmental series. Converted from Gangwayed Brake Van in 1973 to three-phase supply brake generator van for use with HST trailers. Modified 1999 for use with locomotive-hauled stock. B5 bogies. ETS index ??.

Lot No. 30400 Pressed Steel 1958.

6310	(81448, 975325)	**CH**	RV	_RV_	ZG

GENERATOR VAN

Mark 1. Converted from Gangwayed Brake Vans in 1992. B4 (* B5) bogies. ETS index 75.

6311. Lot No. 30162 Pressed Steel 1958. 37.25 t.
6312. Lot No. 30224 Cravens 1956. 37.25 t.
6313. Lot No. 30484 Pressed Steel 1958. 37.25 t.

6311	(80903, 92911)		**CC**	LS	_LS_	CL
6312	(81023, 92925)		**M**	WC	_WC_	CS
6313	(81553, 92167)	*	**PC**	BE	_BP_	SL

BUFFET STANDARD

Mark 2C. Converted from Open Standard by removal of one seating bay and replacing this with a counter with a space for a trolley, now replaced with a more substantial buffet. Adjacent toilet removed and converted to steward's washing area/store. Pressure ventilated. –/55 1T. B4 bogies. ETS 4.

Lot No. 30795 Derby 1969–70. 32.5 t.

6528	(5592)	**M**	WC	_WC_	CS

SLEEPER RECEPTION CAR

Mark 2F. Converted from Open First. These vehicles consist of pantry, microwave cooking facilities, seating area for passengers (with loose chairs, staff toilet plus two bars). Now refurbished again with new "sofa" seating as well as the loose chairs. Converted at RTC, Derby (6700), Ilford (6701–05) and Derby (6706–08). Air conditioned. 6700/01/03/05–08 have Stones equipment and 6702/04 have Temperature Ltd equipment. The number of seats per coach can vary but typically is 25/– 1T (12 seats as "sofa" seating and 13 loose chairs). B4 bogies. d. ETS 5X.

6700–02/04/08. Lot No. 30859 Derby 1973–74. 33.5 t.
6703/05–07. Lot No. 30845 Derby 1973. 33.5 t.

6700	(3347)	**CA**	ER			WO
6701	(3346)	**CA**	CA	*CA*		PO
6702	(3421)	**FS**	CA	*CA*		PO
6703	(3308)	**CA**	ER	*CA*		PO
6704	(3341)	**FS**	CA	*CA*		PO
6705	(3310, 6430)	**FS**	CA	*CA*		PO
6706	(3283, 6421)	**FS**	CA	*CA*		PO
6707	(3276, 6418)	**FS**	CA	*CA*		PO
6708	(3370)	**FS**	CA			WO

BUFFET FIRST

Mark 2D. Converted from Buffet Standard by the removal of another seating bay and fitting a more substantial buffet counter with boiler and microwave oven. Now converted to First Class with new seating and end luggage stacks. Air conditioned. Stones equipment. 30/– 1T. B4 bogies. d. ETS 5. Lot No. 30822 Derby 1971. 33 t.

6723	(5641, 6662)	**M**	WC		CS
6724	(5721, 6665)	**M**	WC	*WC*	CS

OPEN BRAKE STANDARD WITH TROLLEY SPACE

Mark 2. This vehicle uses the same bodyshell as Mark 2 Corridor Brake Firsts and has First Class seat spacing and wider tables. Converted from Open Brake Standard by removal of one seating bay and replacing this with a counter with a space for a trolley. Adjacent toilet removed and converted to a steward's washing area/store. –/23. B4 bogies. ETS 4.

Lot No. 30757 Derby 1966. 31 t.

9101	(9398)	v	**CH**	VT	*VT*		TM

OPEN BRAKE STANDARD

Mark 2. These vehicles use the same bodyshell as Mark 2 Corridor Brake Firsts and have First Class seat spacing and wider tables. Pressure ventilated. –/31 1T. B4 bogies. ETS 4.

9104 was originally numbered 9401. It was renumbered when converted to Open Brake Standard with trolley space. Now returned to original layout.

Lot No. 30757 Derby 1966. 31.5 t.

9104	v	**M**	WC	*WC*	CS		9392	v	**M**	WC	*WC*	CS
9391		**M**	WC	*WC*	CS						

OPEN BRAKE STANDARD

Mark 2D. Air conditioned. Stones Equipment. B4 bogies. d. pg. ETS 5.

* Refurbished with new interior panelling –/31 1T.
s Refurbished with new seating –/22 1TD.

Lot No. 30824 Derby 1971. 33 t.

9479	r	**PC**	LS	*LS*	CL		9493	s	**M**	WC	*WC*	CS
9488	s	**SR**	DR	*SR*	ML						

OPEN BRAKE STANDARD

Mark 2E. Air conditioned. Stones Equipment. Refurbished with new interior panelling. –/32 1T (* –/30 1T 1W). B4 bogies. d. pg. ETS 5.

Lot No. 30838 Derby 1972. 33 t.

Non-standard livery: 9502 Pullman umber & cream.

s Modified design of seat headrest.

9497		**CA**	ER		WO		9507	s	**BG**	RV	*TW*	CF
9502	s	**O**	BE	*BP*	SL		9509	s	**AV**	RV		BU
9504	s*	**BG**	RV	*RV*	BU						

OPEN BRAKE STANDARD

Mark 2F. Air conditioned. Temperature Ltd equipment. All were refurbished in the 1980s with power-operated vestibule doors, new panels and seat rim. All now further refurbished with carpets. –/32 1T (w –/30 1T 1W). B4 bogies. d. pg. ETS 5X.

9537 has had all its seats removed for the purpose of carrying luggage.

Lot No. 30861 Derby 1974. 34 t.

9513		**IC**	ER		WO		9526	n	**BG**	RV	*TW*	CF
9520	nw	**AR**	RV	*TW*	CF		9527	n	**SR**	RV	*SR*	ML
9521		**DS**	RV	*DR*	KM		9537	n	**V**	RV		BU
9525		**DS**	DR	*DR*	KM		9539		**SR**	RV	*SR*	ML

DRIVING OPEN BRAKE STANDARD

Mark 2F. Air conditioned. Temperature Ltd equipment. Push & pull (tdm system). Converted from Open Brake Standard, these vehicles originally had half cabs at the brake end. They have since been refurbished and have had their cabs widened and the cab-end gangways removed. Five vehicles (9701–03/08/14) have been converted for use in Network Rail test trains and can be found in the Service Stock section of this book. –/30(+1) 1W B4 bogies. d. pg. Cowcatchers. ETS 5X.

Lot No. 30861 Derby 1974. Converted Glasgow 1979. Disc brakes. 34 t.

9704	(9512)	**DS**	DR		LW	9709	(9515)	**DS**	DR	LW
9705	(9519)	**DS**	DR	*DR*	KM	9710	(9518)	**DS**	DR	LW
9707	(9511)	**DS**	DR		LW					

OPEN BRAKE UNCLASSIFIED

Mark 2E. Converted from Open Standard with new seating by Railcare Wolverton. Air conditioned. Stones equipment. –/31 2T. B4 bogies. d. ETS 4X.

9800–03. Lot No. 30837 Derby 1972. 33.5 t.
9804–10. Lot No. 30844 Derby 1972–73. 33.5 t.

9800	(5751)	**CA**	ER	*CA*	PO	9806	(5840)	**FS**	CA	*CA*	PO
9801	(5760)	**FS**	CA	*CA*	PO	9807	(5851)	**FS**	ER		WO
9802	(5772)	**CA**	CA	*CA*	PO	9808	(5871)	**FS**	CA		WO
9803	(5799)	**FS**	CA		WO	9809	(5890)	**FS**	CA	*CA*	PO
9804	(5826)	**FS**	CA	*CA*	PO	9810	(5892)	**FS**	CA	*CA*	PO
9805	(5833)	**FS**	CA	*CA*	PO						

KITCHEN BUFFET FIRST

Mark 3A. Air conditioned. Converted from HST catering vehicles and Mark Open Firsts. 18/– plus two seats for staff use (* 24/–, † 35 1T, t 23/– 1T 1W) BT10 bogies. d. ETS 14X.

† Refurbished Great Western Railway Sleeper coaches fitted with new Transcal seating.

Non-standard liveries:

10211 EWS dark maroon.
10241 Livery trials.

10211. Lot No. 30884 Derby 1977. 39.8 t.
10212–229. Lot No. 30878 Derby 1975–76. 39.8 t.
10241–259. Lot No. 30890 Derby 1979. 39.8 t.

10211	(40510)		**0**	DB	*DB*	TO	10229	(11059)	*	**GA**	P	CP
10212	(11049)		**VT**	P		CP	10241	(10009)	*	**0**	P	IL
10217	(11051)	s	**GW**	P	*GW*	PZ	10249	(10012)	t	**AW**	AV	*TW*	CF
10219	(11047)	s	**GW**	P	*GW*	PZ	10259	(10025)	t	**AW**	AV	*TW*	CF
10225	(11014)	s	**GW**	P	*GW*	PZ						

▲ BR blue & grey-liveried Mark 2F Buffet First 1200 is seen near Penzance on 3/04/19.   **Robert Pritchard**

▼ BR carmine & cream-liveried Mark 1 Open First 3068 is seen at Bletchley on 7/07/19.   **Mark Beal**

▲ BR chocolate & cream-liveried Mark 1 Open First 3119 is seen near Craigenhill Summit on 23/09/18. **Robin Ralston**

▼ Royal Train-liveried Royal Kitchen/Household Dining Car 2917 is seen near Symington on 28/06/19. **Robin Ralston**

▲ WCRC maroon-liveried Mark 1 Open First 99125 (3113) is seen at Carlisle on 20/07/19. **Robert Pritchard**

▼ Northern Belle-liveried Open First 3182 "Warwick" is seen at Hanslope Junction on 07/07/19. **Mark Beal**

▲ BR chocolate & cream-liveried Mark 1 Open Standard 4959 is seen at Carlisle on 27/04/19. **Ian Beardsley**

▼ BR blue & grey liveried Mark 2F Open Standard 5961 is seen at Penzance on 13/04/19. **Ian Beardsley**

▲ Revised Direct Rail Services-liveried Mark 2F Open Brake Standard 9525 is seen at Great Yarmouth on 06/08/19. **Robert Pritchard**

▼ Great Western Railway-liveried Mark 3A Sleeping Car with Pantry 10601 is seen at London Paddington on 01/06/19. **Robert Pritchard**

▲ Greater Anglia-liveried Mark 3B Open First 11082 is seen at Norwich on 04/09/19. **Robert Pritchard**

▼ TransPennine Express Mark 5A Open First 11501 is seen Earlestown on 11/09/18. **Alan Hart**

▲ Virgin Trains East Coast-liveried Mark 4 Open First 11426 is seen at Doncaster on 17/06/19. **Robert Pritchard**

▼ Arriva Trains Wales-liveried Mark 3A Open Standard 12184 is seen at Llandudno Junction on 09/08/18. **Robert Pritchard**

▲ Chiltern Railways Mainline-liveried Mark 3A Open Standard 12625 is seen at Dorridge on 20/06/19. **Robert Pritchard**

▼ Caledonian Sleeper Mark 5 Sleeping Car 15333 is seen at Bletchley on 30/06/19. **Mark Bea**

▲ Mark 2B Couchette/Generator Coach 17105 is seen at Cottam Power Station on 28/09/19. **Robert Pritchard**

▼ In Virgin Trains East Coast livery with LNER logos, Mark 4 Driving Brake Van 82223 passes Doncaster leading the 14.30 Edinburgh–London King's Cross on 17/06/19. **Robert Pritchard**

▲ WCRC maroon-liveried Mark 1 Kitchen Car 99316 (converted from Corridor First) is seen at London Euston on 14/07/18. **Tony Christie**

▼ BR carmine & cream-liveried Mark 1 Open Standard 3948, one of the North Yorkshire Moors Railway fleet, is seen at Whitby on 19/04/19. **Ian Beardsley**

▲ In Stagecoach long distance livery with new EMR InterCity logos, HST TKBF is seen at Leicester on 19/08/19. **Robert Pritchard**

▼ CrossCountry-liveried HST TS 42097, fitted with sliding doors, is seen near Rotherham Masborough on 06/06/19. **Robert Pritchard**

▲ ScotRail InterCity-liveried HST Trailer Standard 42292 is seen at Jamestown on 14/07/19. **Robin Ralston**

▼ Great Western Railway-liveried HST Trailer Guard's Standard 49104 is seen at Liskeard on 21/07/19. **Tony Christie**

▲ Royal Scotsman Saloon 99961 "State Car No. 1" is seen near Drem on 05/09/18.   **Robin Ralston**

▼ Pullman-liveried Pullman Parlour Second 348 "TOPAZ" is seen at Totnes on 22/07/18.   **Tony Christie**

▲ BR carmine & cream-liveried Mark 1 Corridor Brake Standard Locomotive Support Coach 35451 is seen at Craigenhill on 18/02/19. **Robin Ralston**

▼ All over dark blue-liveried HST Barrier Vehicle 6340 passes Durham on 04/04/19. **Robert Pritchard**

▲ Arlington Fleet Services-liveried EMU Translator Vehicle 64664 is seen at Great Wymondley, near Hitchin, on 29/06/19.   **Mark Beal**

▼ Network Rail yellow Brake Force Runner 96604 is seen at Norwich on 15/03/19.   **Robert Pritchard**

▲ Network Rail yellow Ultrasonic Test Coach 62287 is seen at Norwich on 15/03/19. **Robert Pritchard**

▼ Network Rail yellow New Measurement Train Lecture Coach 975984 is seen on the approaches to Sheffield on 22/06/19. **Robert Pritchard**

KITCHEN BUFFET FIRST

Mark 3A. Air conditioned. Rebuilt 2011–12 and fitted with sliding plug doors. Interiors originally refurbished for Wrexham & Shropshire with Primarius seating, a new kitchen area and universal-access toilet. Retention toilets. 30/– 1TD 1W. BT10 bogies. ETS 14X.

10271/273/274. Lot No. 30890 Derby 1979. 41.3 t.
10272. Lot No. 30884 Derby 1977. 41.3 t.

10271 (10018, 10236)	**CM**	AV	*CR*	AL
10272 (40517, 10208)	**CM**	AV	*CR*	AL
10273 (10021, 10230)	**CM**	AV	*CR*	AL
10274 (10010, 10255)	**CM**	AV	*CR*	AL

KITCHEN BUFFET STANDARD

Mark 4. Air conditioned. Rebuilt from First to Standard Class with bar adjacent to seating area instead of adjacent to end of coach. Retention toilets. –/30 1T. BT41 bogies. ETS 6X.

Lot No. 31045 Metro-Cammell 1989–92. 43.2 t.

10300	**VE**	E	*LN*	BN	10317	**VE**	E		WS
10301	**VE**	E	*LN*	BN	10318	**VE**	E	*LN*	BN
10302	**VE**	E	*LN*	BN	10319	**VE**	E		WS
10303	**VE**	E	*LN*	BN	10320	**VE**	E	*LN*	BN
10304	**VE**	E	*LN*	BN	10321	**VE**	E	*LN*	BN
10305	**VE**	E	*LN*	BN	10323	**VE**	E	*LN*	BN
10306	**VE**	E	*LN*	BN	10324	**VE**	E	*LN*	BN
10307	**VE**	E	*LN*	BN	10325	**VE**	E		EH
10308	**VE**	E	*LN*	BN	10326	**VE**	E	*LN*	BN
10309	**VE**	E	*LN*	BN	10328	**VE**	E		EH
10310	**VE**	E		BN	10329	**VE**	E		WS
10311	**VE**	E	*LN*	BN	10330	**VE**	E	*LN*	BN
10312	**VE**	E		WS	10331	**VE**	E	*LN*	BN
10313	**VE**	E	*LN*	BN	10332	**VE**	E	*LN*	BN
10315	**VE**	E	*LN*	BN	10333	**VE**	E	*LN*	BN

BUFFET STANDARD

Mark 3A. Air conditioned. Converted from Mark 3 Open Standard at Derby 2006. –/54. d. ETS 13X.

Lot No. 30877 Derby 1975–77. 37.8 t.

10401 (12168)	**GA**	P	*GA*	NC	10404 (12068)	**GA**	P	*GA*	NC
10402 (12010)	**GA**	P	*GA*	NC	10405 (12157)	**GA**	P	*GA*	NC
10403 (12135)	**GA**	P	*GA*	NC	10406 (12020)	**GA**	P	*GA*	NC

BUFFET STANDARD

Mark 3A. Air conditioned. Converted from Mark 3 Kitchen Buffet First 2015–16. –/54. BT10 bogies. d. ETS 13X.

10411–412. Lot No. 30884 Derby 1977. 37.8 t.
10413–416. Lot No. 30878 Derby 1975–76. 37.8 t.
10417. Lot No. 30890 Derby 1979. 37.8 t.

10411 (40519, 10200)	**GA**	P	GA	NC
10412 (40506, 10203)	**GA**	P	GA	NC
10413 (11034, 10214)	**GA**	P	GA	NC
10414 (11041, 10216)	**GA**	P	GA	NC
10415 (11043, 10223)	**GA**	P	GA	NC
10416 (11035, 10228)	**GA**	P	GA	NC
10417 (10011, 10247)	**GA**	P	GA	NC

SLEEPING CAR WITH PANTRY

Mark 3A. Air conditioned. Retention toilets. 12 compartments with a fixed lower berth and a hinged upper berth, plus an attendant's compartment (* 11 compartments with a fixed lower berth and a hinged upper berth + one compartment for a disabled person. 1TD). 2T. BT10 bogies. d. ETS 7X.

Non-standard livery: 10546 EWS dark maroon.

Lot No. 30960 Derby 1981–83. 41 t.

10501	**FS**	P	CA	PO		10561	**FS**	P	CA	PO
10502	**FS**	P	CA	PO		10563	**GW**	P	GW	PZ
10504	**FS**	P	CA	PO		10565	**FS**	P	CA	PO
10513	**FS**	P	CA	PO		10580	**CA**	P	CA	PO
10519	**FS**	P	CA	PO		10584	**GW**	P	GW	PZ
10520	**FS**	P	CA	PO		10589	**GW**	P	GW	PZ
10522	**FS**	P	CA	PO		10590	**GW**	P	GW	PZ
10526	**FS**	P	CA	PO		10594	**GW**	P	GW	PZ
10527	**FS**	P	CA	PO		10596	**GW**	P	GW	PZ
10529	**FS**	P	CA	PO		10597	**FS**	P	CA	PO
10531	**FS**	P	CA	PO		10598	**FS**	P	CA	PO
10532	**GW**	P	GW	PZ		10600	**FS**	P	CA	PO
10534	**GW**	P	GW	PZ		10601 *	**GW**	P	GW	PZ
10542	**FS**	P	CA	PO		10605	**FS**	P	CA	PO
10543	**FS**	P	CA	PO		10607	**FS**	P	CA	PO
10544	**FS**	P	CA	PO		10610	**FS**	P	CA	PO
10546	**0**	DB	DB	TO		10612 *	**GW**	P	GW	PZ
10551	**FS**	P	CA	PO		10614	**FS**	P	CA	PO
10553	**FS**	P	CA	PO		10616 *	**GW**	P	GW	PZ

SLEEPING CAR

Mark 3A. Air conditioned. Retention toilets. 13 compartments with a fixed lower berth and a hinged upper berth (* 11 compartments with a fixed lower berth and a hinged upper berth + one compartment for a disabled person. 1TD). 2T. BT10 bogies. ETS 6X.

10734 was originally 2914 and used as a Royal Train staff sleeping car. It has 12 berths and a shower room and is ETS 11X.

10648–729. Lot No. 30961 Derby 1980–84. 43.5 t.
10734. Lot No. 31002 Derby/Wolverton 1985. 42.5 t.

10648	d*	**FS**	P	*CA*	PO	10699	d*	**FS**	P	*CA*	PO
10650	d*	**FS**	P	*CA*	PO	10703	d	**FS**	P	*CA*	PO
10666	d*	**FS**	P	*CA*	PO	10706	d*	**FS**	P	*CA*	PO
10675	d	**FS**	P	*CA*	PO	10714	d*	**FS**	P	*CA*	PO
10680	d*	**FS**	P	*CA*	PO	10718	d*	**FS**	P	*CA*	PO
10683	d	**FS**	P	*CA*	PO	10719	d*	**FS**	P	*CA*	PO
10688	d	**FS**	P	*CA*	PO	10722	d*	**FS**	P	*CA*	PO
10689	d*	**FS**	P	*CA*	PO	10729		**VN**	WC	*WC*	CS
10690	d	**FS**	P	*CA*	PO	10734		**VN**	WC	*WC*	CS
10693		**CA**	P	*CA*	PO						

Names:

10729	CREWE	10734	BALMORAL

OPEN FIRST

Mark 3A. Air conditioned. All refurbished with table lamps and new seat cushions and trim. 48/– 2T. BT10 bogies. d. ETS 6X.

† Reseated with Standard Class seats: –/68 2T 2W.

11007 was open composite 11907 for a time.

Non-standard livery: 11039 EWS dark maroon.

Lot No. 30878 Derby 1975–76. 34.3 t.

11007		**VT**	P		CP	11031	†	**CM**	AV	*CR*	AL
11018		**VT**	P		CP	11039		**0**	DB	*DB*	TO
11029	†	**CM**	AV	*CR*	AL	11048		**VT**	P		CP

OPEN FIRST

Mark 3B. Air conditioned. InterCity 80 seats. All refurbished with table lamps and new seat cushions and trim. Retention toilets. 48/– 1T. BT10 bogies. d. ETS 6X.

† Fitted with disabled toilet and reduced seating, including three Compin Pegasus seats. 37/– 1TD 2W.

Lot No. 30982 Derby 1985. 36.5 t.

11066	**GA**	P	*GA*	NC	11085 †	**GA**	P	*GA*	NC
11067	**GA**	P	*GA*	NC	11087 †	**GA**	P	*GA*	NC
11068	**GA**	P	*GA*	NC	11088 †	**GA**	P	*GA*	NC
11069	**GA**	P	*GA*	NC	11090 †	**GA**	P	*GA*	NC
11070	**GA**	P	*GA*	NC	11091	**GA**	P	*GA*	NC
11072	**GA**	P	*GA*	NC	11092 †	**GA**	P	*GA*	NC
11073	**GA**	P	*GA*	NC	11093 †	**GA**	P	*GA*	NC
11075	**GA**	P	*GA*	NC	11094 †	**GA**	P	*GA*	NC
11076	**GA**	P	*GA*	NC	11095 †	**GA**	P	*GA*	NC
11077	**GA**	P	*GA*	NC	11096 †	**GA**	P	*GA*	NC
11078 †	**GA**	P	*GA*	NC	11098 †	**GA**	P	*GA*	NC
11080	**GA**	P	*GA*	NC	11099 †	**GA**	P	*GA*	NC
11081	**GA**	P	*GA*	NC	11100 †	**GA**	P	*GA*	NC
11082	**GA**	P	*GA*	NC	11101 †	**GA**	P	*GA*	NC

OPEN FIRST

Mark 4. Air conditioned. Rebuilt with new interior by Bombardier Wakefield 2003–05 (some converted from Standard Class vehicles). Retention toilets. 41/– 1T (plus 2 seats for staff use). BT41 bogies. ETS 6X.

11201–11273. Lot No. 31046 Metro-Cammell 1989–92. 41.3 t.
11277–11299. Lot No. 31049 Metro-Cammell 1989–92. 41.3 t.

11201		**VE**	E	*LN*	BN	11284 (12487)	**VE**	E	*LN*	BN
11219		**VE**	E	*LN*	BN	11285 (12537)	**VE**	E	*LN*	BN
11229		**VE**	E	*LN*	BN	11286 (12482)	**VE**	E	*LN*	BN
11237		**VE**	E		WS	11287 (12527)	**VE**	E	*LN*	BN
11241		**VE**	E	*LN*	BN	11288 (12517)	**VE**	E	*LN*	BN
11244		**VE**	E	*LN*	BN	11289 (12528)	**VE**	E	*LN*	BN
11273		**VE**	E		WS	11290 (12530)	**VE**	E	*LN*	BN
11277 (12408)	**VE**	E	*LN*	BN	11291 (12535)	**VE**	E	*LN*	BN
11278 (12479)	**VE**	E	*LN*	BN	11293 (12536)	**VE**	E		ZB
11279 (12521)	**VE**	E	*LN*	BN	11294 (12529)	**VE**	E		WS
11280 (12523)	**VE**	E	*LN*	BN	11295 (12475)	**VE**	E	*LN*	BN
11281 (12418)	**VE**	E	*LN*	BN	11298 (12416)	**VE**	E	*LN*	BN
11282 (12524)	**VE**	E	*LN*	BN	11299 (12532)	**VE**	E	*LN*	BN
11283 (12435)	**VE**	E	*LN*	BN					

OPEN FIRST (DISABLED)

Mark 4. Air conditioned. Rebuilt from Open First by Bombardier Wakefield 2003–05. Retention toilets. 42/– 1TD 1W. BT41 bogies. ETS 6X.

Lot No. 31046 Metro-Cammell 1989–92. 40.7 t.

11301 (11215)	**VE**	E	*LN*	BN	11307 (11217)	**VE**	E	*LN*	BN
11302 (11203)	**VE**	E	*LN*	BN	11308 (11263)	**VE**	E	*LN*	BN
11303 (11211)	**VE**	E	*LN*	BN	11309 (11259)	**VE**	E	*LN*	BN
11304 (11257)	**VE**	E	*LN*	BN	11310 (11272)	**VE**	E	*LN*	BN
11305 (11261)	**VE**	E	*LN*	BN	11311 (11221)	**VE**	E	*LN*	BN
11306 (11276)	**VE**	E	*LN*	BN	11312 (11225)	**VE**	E	*LN*	BN

11313	(11210)	**VE**	E	*LN*	BN	11322	(11228)	**VE**	E	*LN* BN
11314	(11207)	**VE**	E	*LN*	BN	11323	(11235)	**VE**	E	EH
11315	(11238)	**VE**	E	*LN*	BN	11324	(11253)	**VE**	E	EH
11316	(11227)	**VE**	E	*LN*	BN	11325	(11231)	**VE**	E	WS
11317	(11223)	**VE**	E	*LN*	BN	11326	(11206)	**VE**	E	*LN* BN
11318	(11251)	**VE**	E	*LN*	BN	11327	(11236)	**VE**	E	WS
11319	(11247)	**VE**	E	*LN*	BN	11328	(11274)	**VE**	E	WS
11320	(11255)	**VE**	E	*LN*	BN	11329	(11243)	**VE**	E	WS
11321	(11245)	**VE**	E	*LN*	BN	11330	(11249)	**VE**	E	WS

OPEN FIRST

Mark 4. Air conditioned. Rebuilt from Open First by Bombardier Wakefield 2003–05. Separate area for 7 smokers, although smoking is no longer allowed. Retention toilets. 46/– 1TD 1W. BT41 bogies. ETS 6X.

Lot No. 31046 Metro-Cammell 1989–92. 42.1 t.

11401	(11214)	**VE**	E	*LN*	BN	11416	(11254)	**VE**	E	*LN* BN
11402	(11216)	**VE**	E	*LN*	BN	11417	(11226)	**VE**	E	*LN* BN
11403	(11258)	**VE**	E	*LN*	BN	11418	(11222)	**VE**	E	*LN* BN
11404	(11202)	**VE**	E	*LN*	BN	11419	(11250)	**VE**	E	*LN* BN
11405	(11204)	**VE**	E	*LN*	BN	11420	(11242)	**VE**	E	*LN* BN
11406	(11205)	**VE**	E	*LN*	BN	11421	(11220)	**VE**	E	*LN* BN
11407	(11256)	**VE**	E	*LN*	BN	11422	(11232)	**VE**	E	*LN* BN
11408	(11218)	**VE**	E	*LN*	BN	11424	(11239)	**VE**	E	ZB
11409	(11262)	**VE**	E	*LN*	BN	11425	(11234)	**VE**	E	WS
11410	(11260)	**VE**	E	*LN*	BN	11426	(11252)	**VE**	E	*LN* BN
11411	(11240)	**VE**	E	*LN*	BN	11427	(11200)	**VE**	E	WS
11412	(11209)	**VE**	E	*LN*	BN	11428	(11233)	**VE**	E	WS
11413	(11212)	**VE**	E	*LN*	BN	11429	(11275)	**VE**	E	WS
11414	(11246)	**VE**	E	*LN*	BN	11430	(11248)	**VE**	E	WS
11415	(11208)	**VE**	E	*LN*	BN					

OPEN FIRST

CAF Mark 5A. Air conditioned. Currently entering service with TransPennine Express. Retention toilets. 30/– 1TD 2W. CAF bogies. ETS XX.

CAF Beasain 2017–18. 32.7 t.

11501	**TP**	BN		LW	11508	**TP**	BN		MA
11502	**TP**	BN		LW	11509	**TP**	BN	*TP*	MA
11503	**TP**	BN		LW	11510	**TP**	BN		
11504	**TP**	BN	*TP*	MA	11511	**TP**	BN	*TP*	MA
11505	**TP**	BN		LW	11512	**TP**	BN	*TP*	MA
11506	**TP**	BN	*TP*	MA	11513	**TP**	BN		LW
11507	**TP**	BN		MA					

OPEN FIRST

Mark 4. Air conditioned. Converted from Kitchen Buffet Standard with new interior by Bombardier Wakefield 2005. Retention toilets. 46/– 1T. BT41 bogies. ETS 6X.

Lot No. 31046 Metro-Cammell 1989–92. 41.3 t.

| 11998 (10314) | **VE** | E | | WS | | 11999 (10316) | **VE** | E | | WS |

OPEN STANDARD

Mark 3A. Air conditioned. All refurbished with modified seat backs and new layout and further refurbished with new seat trim. –/76 2T († –/70 2T 1W, t –/72 2T, z –/70 1TD 1T 2W). BT10 bogies. d. ETS 6X.

* Further refurbished with more unidirectional seating and one toilet removed. Retention toilets. –/80 1T.

s Refurbished Sleeper day coaches fitted with new Transcal seating to a 2+2 layout and a universal access toilet. Retention toilets. –/65 1TD 1W.

12170/171 were converted from Open Composites 11909/910, formerly Open Firsts 11009/010.

12005–167. Lot No. 30877 Derby 1975–77. 34.3 t.
12170/171. Lot No. 30878 Derby 1975–76. 34.3 t.

12005	*	**GA**	P	*GA*	NC	12051	*	**GA**	P	*GA*	NC
12009	*	**GA**	P	*GA*	NC	12054	†	**CM**	AV	*CR*	AL
12011		**VT**	P		CP	12056	*	**GA**	P	*GA*	NC
12012	*	**GA**	P	*GA*	NC	12057	*	**GA**	P	*GA*	NC
12013	*	**GA**	P	*GA*	NC	12060	*	**GA**	P	*GA*	NC
12015	*	**GA**	P	*GA*	NC	12061	*	**GA**	P	*GA*	NC
12016	*	**GA**	P	*GA*	NC	12062	*	**GA**	P	*GA*	NC
12017	t	**CM**	AV	*CR*	AL	12064	*	**GA**	P	*GA*	NC
12019	*	**GA**	P	*GA*	NC	12066	*	**GA**	P	*GA*	NC
12021	*	**GA**	P	*GA*	NC	12067	*	**GA**	P	*GA*	NC
12024	*	**GA**	P	*GA*	NC	12073	*	**GA**	P	*GA*	NC
12026	*	**GA**	P	*GA*	NC	12078		**VT**	P		CP
12027	*	**GA**	P	*GA*	NC	12079	*	**GA**	P	*GA*	NC
12030	*	**GA**	P	*GA*	NC	12081	*	**GA**	P	*GA*	NC
12031	*	**GA**	P	*GA*	NC	12082	*	**GA**	P	*GA*	NC
12032	*	**GA**	P	*GA*	NC	12084	*	**GA**	P	*GA*	NC
12034	*	**GA**	P	*GA*	NC	12089	*	**GA**	P	*GA*	NC
12035	*	**GA**	P	*GA*	NC	12090	*	**GA**	P	*GA*	NC
12036	†	**CM**	AV	*CR*	AL	12091	*	**GA**	P	*GA*	NC
12037	*	**GA**	P	*GA*	NC	12093	*	**GA**	P	*GA*	NC
12040	*	**GA**	P	*GA*	NC	12094		**CM**	AV	*CR*	AL
12041	*	**GA**	P	*GA*	NC	12097	*	**GA**	P	*GA*	NC
12042	*	**GA**	P	*GA*	NC	12098	*	**GA**	P	*GA*	NC
12043	†	**CM**	AV	*CR*	AL	12099	*	**GA**	P	*GA*	NC
12046	*	**GA**	P	*GA*	NC	12100	s	**GW**	P	*GW*	PZ
12049	*	**GA**	P	*GA*	NC	12103	*	**GA**	P	*GA*	NC

12105	*	**GA**	P	*GA*	NC	12138		**VT**	P		CP
12107	*	**GA**	P	*GA*	NC	12139	*	**GA**	P	*GA*	NC
12108	*	**GA**	P	*GA*	NC	12141	*	**GA**	P	*GA*	NC
12109	*	**GA**	P	*GA*	NC	12142	s	**GW**	P	*GW*	PZ
12110	*	**GA**	P	*GA*	NC	12143	*	**GA**	P	*GA*	NC
12111	*	**GA**	P	*GA*	NC	12146	*	**GA**	P	*GA*	NC
12114	*	**GA**	P	*GA*	NC	12147	*	**GA**	P	*GA*	NC
12115	*	**GA**	P	*GA*	NC	12148	*	**GA**	P	*GA*	NC
12116	*	**GA**	P	*GA*	NC	12150	*	**GA**	P	*GA*	NC
12118	*	**GA**	P	*GA*	NC	12151	*	**GA**	P	*GA*	NC
12119	t	**CM**	AV	*CR*	AL	12153	*	**GA**	P	*GA*	NC
12120	*	**GA**	P	*GA*	NC	12154	*	**GA**	P	*GA*	NC
12122	z	**VT**	P		CP	12159	*	**GA**	P	*GA*	NC
12125	*	**GA**	P	*GA*	NC	12161	s	**GW**	P	*GW*	PZ
12126	*	**GA**	P	*GA*	NC	12164	*	**GA**	P	*GA*	NC
12129	*	**GA**	P	*GA*	NC	12166	*	**GA**	P	*GA*	NC
12130	*	**GA**	P	*GA*	NC	12167	*	**GA**	P	*GA*	NC
12132	*	**GA**	P	*GA*	NC	12170	*	**GA**	P	*GA*	NC
12133		**VT**	P		CP	12171	*	**GA**	P	*GA*	NC
12137	*	**GA**	P	*GA*	NC						

OPEN STANDARD

Mark 3A (†) or Mark 3B. Air conditioned. Converted from Mark 3A or 3B Open First. Fitted with new Grammer seating. –/70 2T 1W. BT10 bogies. d. ETS 6X.

12176–181/185. Mark 3B. Lot No. 30982 Derby 1985. 38.5 t.
12182–184. Mark 3A. Lot No. 30878 Derby 1975–76. 38.5 t.

12176	(11064)		**AW**	AV	*TW*	CF
12177	(11065)		**AW**	AV	*TW*	CF
12178	(11071)		**AW**	AV	*TW*	CF
12179	(11083)		**AW**	AV	*TW*	CF
12180	(11084)		**AW**	AV	*TW*	CF
12181	(11086)		**AW**	AV	*TW*	CF
12182	(11013)	†	**AW**	AV	*TW*	CF
12183	(11027)	†	**AW**	AV	*TW*	CF
12184	(11044)	†	**AW**	AV	*TW*	CF
12185	(11089)		**AW**	AV	*TW*	CF

OPEN STANDARD (END)

Mark 4. Air conditioned. Rebuilt with new interior by Bombardier Wakefield 2003–05. Separate area for 26 smokers, although smoking is no longer allowed. Retention toilets. –/76 1T. BT41 bogies. ETS 6X.

12232 was converted from the original 12405.

12200–231. Lot No. 31047 Metro-Cammell 1989–91. 39.5 t.
12232. Lot No. 31049 Metro-Cammell 1989–92. 39.5 t.

12200	**VE**	E	*LN*	BN	12217	**VE**	E		WS
12201	**VE**	E	*LN*	BN	12218	**VE**	E		BN
12202	**VE**	E	*LN*	BN	12219	**VE**	E		EH
12203	**VE**	E	*LN*	BN	12220	**VE**	E	*LN*	BN
12204	**VE**	E		WS	12222	**VE**	E	*LN*	BN
12205	**VE**	E	*LN*	BN	12223	**VE**	E	*LN*	BN
12207	**VE**	E	*LN*	BN	12224	**VE**	E	*LN*	BN
12208	**VE**	E	*LN*	BN	12225	**VE**	E		EH
12209	**VE**	E	*LN*	BN	12226	**VE**	E	*LN*	BN
12210	**VE**	E	*LN*	BN	12227	**VE**	E		WS
12211	**VE**	E	*LN*	BN	12228	**VE**	E	*LN*	BN
12212	**VE**	E	*LN*	BN	12229	**VE**	E	*LN*	BN
12213	**VE**	E	*LN*	BN	12230	**VE**	E	*LN*	BN
12214	**VE**	E	*LN*	BN	12231	**VE**	E	*LN*	BN
12215	**VE**	E	*LN*	BN	12232	**VE**	E	*LN*	BN
12216	**VE**	E		WS					

OPEN STANDARD (DISABLED)

Mark 4. Air conditioned. Rebuilt with new interior by Bombardier Wakefield 2003–05. Retention toilets. –/68 2W 1TD. BT41 bogies. ETS 6X.

12331 was converted from Open Standard 12531.

12300–330. Lot No. 31048 Metro-Cammell 1989–91. 39.4 t.
12331. Lot No. 31049 Metro-Cammell 1989–92. 39.4 t.

12300	**VE**	E	*LN*	BN	12317	**VE**	E		WS
12301	**VE**	E	*LN*	BN	12318	**VE**	E		WS
12302	**VE**	E	*LN*	BN	12319	**VE**	E		ZB
12303	**VE**	E	*LN*	BN	12320	**VE**	E		BN
12304	**VE**	E	*LN*	BN	12321	**VE**	E		WS
12305	**VE**	E	*LN*	BN	12322	**VE**	E		WS
12307	**VE**	E	*LN*	BN	12323	**VE**	E	*LN*	BN
12308	**VE**	E	*LN*	BN	12324	**VE**	E	*LN*	BN
12309	**VE**	E	*LN*	BN	12325	**VE**	E	*LN*	BN
12310	**VE**	E	*LN*	BN	12326	**VE**	E	*LN*	BN
12311	**VE**	E	*LN*	BN	12327	**VE**	E	*LN*	BN
12312	**VE**	E	*LN*	BN	12328	**VE**	E	*LN*	BN
12313	**VE**	E	*LN*	BN	12329	**VE**	E	*LN*	BN
12315	**VE**	E	*LN*	BN	12330	**VE**	E	*LN*	BN
12316	**VE**	E	*LN*	BN	12331	**VE**	E		WS

OPEN STANDARD

Mark 4. Air conditioned. Rebuilt with new interior by Bombardier Wakefield 2003–05. Retention toilets. –/76 1T. BT41 bogies. ETS 6X.

12405 is the second coach to carry that number. It was built from the bodyshell originally intended for 12221. The original 12405 is now 12232.

Lot No. 31049 Metro-Cammell 1989–92. 40.8 t.

No.					No.				
12400	**VE**	E	*LN*	BN	12450	**VE**	E	*LN*	BN
12401	**VE**	E	*LN*	BN	12452	**VE**	E	*LN*	BN
12402	**VE**	E	*LN*	BN	12453	**VE**	E	*LN*	BN
12403	**VE**	E		ZB	12454	**VE**	E		EH
12404	**VE**	E	*LN*	BN	12457	**VE**	E		WS
12405	**VE**	E	*LN*	BN	12458	**VE**	E		WS
12406	**VE**	E	*LN*	BN	12459	**VE**	E	*LN*	BN
12407	**VE**	E	*LN*	BN	12460	**VE**	E	*LN*	BN
12409	**VE**	E	*LN*	BN	12461	**VE**	E	*LN*	BN
12410	**VE**	E	*LN*	BN	12462	**VE**	E		WS
12411	**VE**	E	*LN*	BN	12463	**VE**	E		WS
12414	**VE**	E	*LN*	BN	12464	**VE**	E		WS
12415	**VE**	E	*LN*	BN	12465	**VE**	E	*LN*	BN
12417	**VE**	E	*LN*	BN	12466	**VE**	E		WS
12419	**VE**	E	*LN*	BN	12467	**VE**	E	*LN*	BN
12420	**VE**	E	*LN*	BN	12468	**VE**	E	*LN*	BN
12421	**VE**	E	*LN*	BN	12469	**VE**	E	*LN*	BN
12422	**VE**	E	*LN*	BN	12470	**VE**	E	*LN*	BN
12423	**VE**	E	*LN*	BN	12471	**VE**	E		WS
12424	**VE**	E	*LN*	BN	12472	**VE**	E		WS
12425	**VE**	E		ZB	12473	**VE**	E	*LN*	BN
12426	**VE**	E	*LN*	BN	12474	**VE**	E	*LN*	BN
12427	**VE**	E	*LN*	BN	12476	**VE**	E	*LN*	BN
12428	**VE**	E	*LN*	BN	12477	**VE**	E	*LN*	BN
12429	**VE**	E	*LN*	BN	12478	**VE**	E	*LN*	BN
12430	**VE**	E	*LN*	BN	12480	**VE**	E	*LN*	BN
12431	**VE**	E	*LN*	BN	12481	**VE**	E	*LN*	BN
12432	**VE**	E	*LN*	BN	12483	**VE**	E	*LN*	BN
12433	**VE**	E	*LN*	BN	12484	**VE**	E	*LN*	BN
12434	**VE**	E	*LN*	BN	12485	**VE**	E	*LN*	BN
12436	**VE**	E	*LN*	BN	12486	**VE**	E	*LN*	BN
12437	**VE**	E	*LN*	BN	12488	**VE**	E	*LN*	BN
12438	**VE**	E		WS	12489	**VE**	E	*LN*	BN
12439	**VE**	E	*LN*	BN	12513	**VE**	E	*LN*	BN
12440	**VE**	E	*LN*	BN	12514	**VE**	E	*LN*	BN
12441	**VE**	E	*LN*	BN	12515	**VE**	E	*LN*	BN
12442	**VE**	E	*LN*	BN	12518	**VE**	E	*LN*	BN
12443	**VE**	E	*LN*	BN	12519	**VE**	E		WS
12444	**VE**	E	*LN*	BN	12520	**VE**	E	*LN*	BN
12445	**VE**	E	*LN*	BN	12522	**VE**	E	*LN*	BN
12446	**VE**	E		WS	12526	**VE**	E	*LN*	BN
12447	**VE**	E		EH	12533	**VE**	E		WS
12448	**VE**	E	*LN*	BN	12534	**VE**	E		WS
12449	**VE**	E		WS	12538	**VE**	E		WS

OPEN STANDARD

Mark 3A. Air conditioned. Rebuilt 2011–13 and fitted with sliding plug doors. Original InterCity 70 seating retained but mainly arranged around tables. Retention toilets. –/72(+6) or * –/69(+4) 1T. BT10 bogies. ETS 6X.

12602–609/614–616/618/620. Lot No. 30877 Derby 1975–77. 36.2 t (* 37.1 t).
12601/613/617–619/621/623/625/627. Lot No. 30878 Derby 1975–76. 36.2 t (* 37.1 t).

12602	(12072)		**CM**	AV	*CR*	AL
12603	(12053)	*	**CM**	AV	*CR*	AL
12604	(12131)		**CM**	AV	*CR*	AL
12605	(11040)	*	**CM**	AV	*CR*	AL
12606	(12048)		**CM**	AV	*CR*	AL
12607	(12038)	*	**CM**	AV	*CR*	AL
12608	(12069)		**CM**	AV	*CR*	AL
12609	(12014)	*	**CM**	AV	*CR*	AL
12610	(12117)		**CM**	AV	*CR*	AL
12613	(11042, 12173)	*	**CM**	AV	*CR*	AL
12614	(12145)		**CM**	AV	*CR*	AL
12615	(12059)	*	**CM**	AV	*CR*	AL
12616	(12127)		**CM**	AV	*CR*	AL
12617	(11052, 12174)	*	**CM**	AV	*CR*	AL
12618	(11008, 12169)		**CM**	AV	*CR*	AL
12619	(11058, 12175)	*	**CM**	AV	*CR*	AL
12620	(12124)		**CM**	AV	*CR*	AL
12621	(11046)	*	**CM**	AV	*CR*	AL
12623	(11019)	*	**CM**	AV	*CR*	AL
12625	(11030)	*	**CM**	AV	*CR*	AL
12627	(11054)	*	**CM**	AV	*CR*	AL

OPEN STANDARD

CAF Mark 5A. Air conditioned. Currently entering service with TransPennine Express. Retention toilets. –/69 1T (* –/59(+6) 1T + bike spaces). CAF bogies. ETS XX.

CAF Beasain 2017–18. 31.8 t (* 31.6 t).

12701		**TP**	BN		LW	12713		**TP**	BN		LW
12702		**TP**	BN		LW	12714		**TP**	BN		LW
12703	*	**TP**	BN		LW	12715	*	**TP**	BN		LW
12704		**TP**	BN		LW	12716		**TP**	BN	*TP*	MA
12705		**TP**	BN		LW	12717		**TP**	BN	*TP*	MA
12706	*	**TP**	BN		LW	12718	*	**TP**	BN	*TP*	MA
12707		**TP**	BN		LW	12719		**TP**	BN		MA
12708		**TP**	BN		LW	12720		**TP**	BN		MA
12709	*	**TP**	BN		LW	12721	*	**TP**	BN		MA
12710		**TP**	BN	*TP*	MA	12722		**TP**	BN		MA
12711		**TP**	BN	*TP*	MA	12723		**TP**	BN		MA
12712	*	**TP**	BN	*TP*	MA	12724	*	**TP**	BN		MA

12725	**TP**	BN	*TP*	MA
12726	**TP**	BN	*TP*	MA
12727 *	**TP**	BN	*TP*	MA
12728	**TP**	BN		
12729	**TP**	BN		
12730 *	**TP**	BN		
12731	**TP**	BN	*TP*	MA
12732	**TP**	BN	*TP*	MA

12733 *	**TP**	BN	*TP*	MA
12734	**TP**	BN	*TP*	MA
12735	**TP**	BN	*TP*	MA
12736 *	**TP**	BN	*TP*	MA
12737	**TP**	BN		MA
12738	**TP**	BN		MA
12739 *	**TP**	BN		MA

DRIVING OPEN BRAKE STANDARD

CAF Mark 5A. Air conditioned. Currently entering service with TransPennine Express. Retention toilets. –/64. CAF bogies. ETS XX.

CAF Irun 2017–18. 32.9 t.

12801	**TP**	BN		LW
12802	**TP**	BN		LW
12803	**TP**	BN		LW
12804	**TP**	BN	*TP*	MA
12805	**TP**	BN		LW
12806	**TP**	BN	*TP*	MA
12807	**TP**	BN		MA

12808	**TP**	BN		MA
12809	**TP**	BN	*TP*	MA
12810	**TP**	BN		
12811	**TP**	BN	*TP*	MA
12812	**TP**	BN	*TP*	MA
12813	**TP**	BN		MA
12814	**TP**	BN		

CORRIDOR FIRST

Mark 1. Seven compartments. 42/– 2T. B4 bogies. ETS 3.

Lot No. 30381 Swindon 1959. 33 t.

13227 x	**CC**	LS	*LS*	CL
13229 xk	**M**	SP	*SP*	BO

13230 xk	**M**	SP	*SP*	BO

OPEN FIRST

Mark 1 converted from Corridor First in 2013–14. 42/– 2T. Commonwealth bogies. ETS 3.

Lot No. 30667 Swindon 1962. 35 t.

13320 x	**M**	WC	*WC*	CS	ANNA

CORRIDOR FIRST

Mark 2A. Seven compartments. Pressure ventilated. 42/– 2T. B4 bogies. ETS 4.

Lot No. 30774 Derby 1968. 33 t.

13440 v	**M**	WC	*WC*	CS

SLEEPER SEATED CARRIAGE WITH BRAKE

CAF Mark 5. Air conditioned. Retention toilets. –/31 1TD 1W. CAF bogies. ETS XX.

CAF Irun 2016–18. 32.5 t.

15001	**CA** LF	*CA*	PO	15007	**CA** LF	*CA*	PO
15002	**CA** LF	*CA*	PO	15008	**CA** LF	*CA*	PO
15003	**CA** LF	*CA*	PO	15009	**CA** LF	*CA*	PO
15004	**CA** LF	*CA*	PO	15010	**CA** LF	*CA*	PO
15005	**CA** LF	*CA*	PO	15011	**CA** LF	*CA*	PO
15006	**CA** LF	*CA*	PO				

SLEEPER LOUNGE CAR

CAF Mark 5. Air conditioned. –/30 or –/28 1W. CAF bogies. ETS XX.

CAF Beasain 2016–18. 35.5 t.

15101	**CA** LF	*CA*	PO	15106	**CA** LF	*CA*	PO
15102	**CA** LF	*CA*	PO	15107	**CA** LF	*CA*	PO
15103	**CA** LF	*CA*	PO	15108	**CA** LF	*CA*	PO
15104	**CA** LF	*CA*	PO	15109	**CA** LF	*CA*	PO
15105	**CA** LF	*CA*	PO	15110	**CA** LF	*CA*	PO

SLEEPING CAR (FULLY ACCESSIBLE)

CAF Mark 5. Air conditioned. Retention toilets. Two fully accessible berths (one with double bed, one with foldable upper bed), two berths with double beds and en-suite toilets and showers, two berths with foldable upper beds. 2TD 2T, plus two showers. CAF bogies. ETS XX.

CAF Castejon/Irun 2016–18. 35.5 t.

15201	**CA** LF	*CA*	PO	15208	**CA** LF	*CA*	PO
15202	**CA** LF	*CA*	PO	15209	**CA** LF	*CA*	PO
15203	**CA** LF	*CA*	PO	15210	**CA** LF	*CA*	PO
15204	**CA** LF	*CA*	PO	15211	**CA** LF	*CA*	PO
15205	**CA** LF	*CA*	PO	15212	**CA** LF	*CA*	PO
15206	**CA** LF	*CA*	PO	15213	**CA** LF	*CA*	PO
15207	**CA** LF	*CA*	PO	15214	**CA** LF	*CA*	PO

SLEEPING CAR

CAF Mark 5. Air conditioned. Retention toilets. 6 en-suite toilet/shower and 4 non en-suite compartments with a fixed lower berth and hinged upper berth. 7T. CAF bogies. ETS XX.

CAF Beasain 2016–18. 38.0 t.

15301	**CA** LF	*CA*	PO	15303	**CA** LF	*CA*	PO
15302	**CA** LF	*CA*	PO	15304	**CA** LF	*CA*	PO

15305	**CA** LF	*CA*	PO		15323	**CA** LF	*CA*	PO
15306	**CA** LF	*CA*	PO		15324	**CA** LF	*CA*	PO
15307	**CA** LF	*CA*	PO		15325	**CA** LF	*CA*	PO
15308	**CA** LF	*CA*	PO		15326	**CA** LF	*CA*	PO
15309	**CA** LF	*CA*	PO		15327	**CA** LF	*CA*	PO
15310	**CA** LF	*CA*	PO		15328	**CA** LF	*CA*	PO
15311	**CA** LF	*CA*	PO		15329	**CA** LF	*CA*	PO
15312	**CA** LF	*CA*	PO		15330	**CA** LF	*CA*	PO
15313	**CA** LF	*CA*	PO		15331	**CA** LF	*CA*	PO
15314	**CA** LF	*CA*	PO		15332	**CA** LF	*CA*	PO
15315	**CA** LF	*CA*	PO		15333	**CA** LF	*CA*	PO
15316	**CA** LF	*CA*	PO		15334	**CA** LF	*CA*	PO
15317	**CA** LF	*CA*	PO		15335	**CA** LF	*CA*	PO
15318	**CA** LF	*CA*	PO		15336	**CA** LF	*CA*	PO
15319	**CA** LF	*CA*	PO		15337	**CA** LF	*CA*	PO
15320	**CA** LF	*CA*	PO		15338	**CA** LF	*CA*	PO
15321	**CA** LF	*CA*	PO		15339	**CA** LF	*CA*	PO
15322	**CA** LF	*CA*	PO		15340	**CA** LF	*CA*	PO

CORRIDOR BRAKE FIRST

Mark 1. Four compartments. 24/– 1T. Commonwealth bogies. ETS 2.

Lot No. 30668 Swindon 1961. 36 t.

17018	(14018)	v	**CH** VT		TM	BOTAURUS

CORRIDOR BRAKE FIRST

Mark 2A. Four compartments. Pressure ventilated. 24/– 1T. B4 bogies. ETS 4.

17080/090 were numbered 35516/503 for a time when declassified.

17056. Lot No. 30775 Derby 1967–68. 32 t.
17080–102. Lot No. 30786 Derby 1968. 32 t.

17056	(14056)		**CC** LS		ZG
17080	(14080)		**PC** LS		ZG
17090	(14090)	v	**CH** VT		TM
17102	(14102)		**M** WC	*WC*	CS

COUCHETTE/GENERATOR COACH

Mark 2B. Formerly part of Royal Train. Converted from Corridor Brake First built 1969. Consists of luggage accommodation, guard's compartment, 350 kW diesel generator and staff sleeping accommodation. Pressure ventilated. B5 bogies. ETS 5X (when generator not in use). ETS index ?? (when generator in use).

Lot No. 30888 Wolverton 1977. 46 t.

17105	(14105, 2905)	**BG** RV	*RV*	BU

CORRIDOR BRAKE FIRST

Mark 2D. Four compartments. Air conditioned. Stones equipment. 24/– 1T. B4 Bogies. ETS 5.

Lot No. 30823 Derby 1971–72. 33.5 t.

17159	(14159)	d	**CC**	LS	*LS*		CL	
17167	(14167)		**VN**	WC	*WC*		CS	MOW COP

OPEN BRAKE UNCLASSIFIED

Mark 3B. Air conditioned. Fitted with hydraulic handbrake. Used as Sleeper day coaches. Refurbished with new Transcal seating 2018. 55/– 1T. BT10 bogies. pg. d. ETS 6X.

Lot No. 30990 Derby 1986. 35.8 t.

17173	**GW**	P	*GW*	PZ		17175	**GW**	P	*GW*	PZ
17174	**GW**	P	*GW*	PZ						

CORRIDOR STANDARD

Mark 1. –/48 2T. Eight Compartments. Commonwealth bogies. ETS 4.

Currently in use as part of the Harry Potter World exhibition at Leavesden, near Watford.

Lot No. 30685 Derby 1961–62. 36 t.

18756	(25756)	x	**M**	WC		SH

CORRIDOR BRAKE COMPOSITE

Mark 1. There are two variants depending upon whether the Standard Class compartments have armrests. Each vehicle has two First Class and three Standard Class compartments. 12/18 2T (* 12/24 2T). Commonwealth bogies. ETS 2.

21241–245. Lot No. 30669 Swindon 1961–62. 36 t.
21256. Lot No. 30731 Derby 1963. 37 t.
21266–272. Lot No. 30732 Derby 1964. 37 t.

21241	x	**M**	SP	*SP*	BO		21266	x*	**M**	WC	*WC*	CS
21245	x	**M**	RV		ZG		21269	*	**CC**	RV	*RV*	ZG
21256	x	**M**	WC	*WC*	CS		21272	x*	**CH**	RV	*RV*	ZG

CORRIDOR BRAKE STANDARD

Mark 1. Four compartments. –/24 1T. ETS 2.

35185. Lot No. 30427 Wolverton 1959. B4 bogies. 33 t.
35459/465. Lot No. 30721 Wolverton 1963. Commonwealth bogies. 37 t.

35185	x	**M**	SP	*SP*	BO
35459	x	**M**	WC	*WC*	CS
35465	x	**CC**	LS	*LS*	CL

CORRIDOR BRAKE GENERATOR STANDARD

Mark 1. Four compartments. –/24 1T. Fitted with an ETS generator in the former luggage compartment. ETS 2 (when generator not in use). ETS index ?? (when generator in use).

Lot No. 30721 Wolverton 1963. Commonwealth bogies. 37 t.

| 35469 | x | **CH** | RV | *RV* | ZG |

BRAKE/POWER KITCHEN

Mark 2C. Pressure ventilated. Converted from Corridor Brake First (declassified to Corridor Brake Standard) built 1970. Converted by West Coast Railway Company 2000–01. Consists of 60 kVA generator, guard's compartment and electric kitchen. ETS ? (when generator not in use). ETS index ?? (when generator in use).

Non-standard livery: Brown.

Lot No. 30796 Derby 1969–70. 32.5 t.

| 35511 | (14130, 17130) | | **0** | LS | | CL |

KITCHEN CAR

Mark 1. Converted 1989/2006/2017–19 from Kitchen Buffet Unclassified. 80041/020 had buffet and seating area replaced with additional kitchen and food preparation area. 80043 had a full length kitchen fitted. Fluorescent lighting. Commonwealth or (†) B5 bogies. ETS 2X.

Lot No. 30628 Pressed Steel 1960–61. 39 t (* 36.4 t).

80041	(1690)	x	**M**	RV		ZG
80042	(1646)		**CH**	RV	*RV*	ZG
80043	(1680)	*	**PC**	LS	*LS*	CL
80044	(1659)	†	**CC**	LS	*LS*	CL

DRIVING BRAKE VAN (110 mph)

Mark 3B. Air conditioned. T4 bogies. dg. ETS 5X. Driving Brake Vans converted for use by Network Rail can be found in the Service Stock section of this book.

Non-standard livery: 82146 All over silver with DB logos.

Lot No. 31042 Derby 1988. 45.2 t.

| 82102 | **GA** | P | *GA* | NC | 82105 | **GA** | P | *GA* | NC |
| 82103 | **GA** | P | *GA* | NC | 82107 | **GA** | P | *GA* | NC |

82112	**GA**	P	*GA*	NC		82133	**GA**	P	*GA*	NC
82114	**GA**	P	*GA*	NC		82136	**GA**	P	*GA*	NC
82118	**GA**	P	*GA*	NC		82139	**GA**	P	*GA*	NC
82121	**GA**	P	*GA*	NC		82143	**GA**	P	*GA*	NC
82127	**GA**	P	*GA*	NC		82146	**0**	DB	*DB*	TO
82132	**GA**	P	*GA*	NC		82152	**GA**	P	*GA*	NC

DRIVING BRAKE VAN (140 mph)

Mark 4. Air conditioned. Swiss-built (SIG) bogies. dg. ETS 6X.

Advertising livery: 82205 Flying Scotsman (red, white & purple).

Lot No. 31043 Metro-Cammell 1988. 43.5 t.

82200	**VE**	E	*LN*	BN		82216	**VE**	E		WS
82201	**VE**	E	*LN*	BN		82217	**VE**	E	*LN*	BN
82202	**VE**	E	*LN*	BN		82218	**VE**	E	*LN*	BN
82203	**VE**	E		WS		82219	**VE**	E	*LN*	BN
82204	**VE**	E	*LN*	BN		82220	**VE**	E	*LN*	BN
82205	**AL**	E	*LN*	BN		82222	**VE**	E	*LN*	BN
82206	**VE**	E	*LN*	BN		82223	**VE**	E	*LN*	BN
82207	**VE**	E	*LN*	BN		82224	**VE**	E	*LN*	BN
82208	**VE**	E	*LN*	BN		82225	**VE**	E	*LN*	BN
82209	**VE**	E	*LN*	BN		82226	**VE**	E		EH
82210	**VE**	E	*LN*	BN		82227	**VE**	E	*LN*	BN
82211	**VE**	E	*LN*	BN		82228	**VE**	E		WS
82212	**VE**	E	*LN*	BN		82229	**VE**	E		EH
82213	**VE**	E	*LN*	BN		82230	**VE**	E	*LN*	BN
82214	**VE**	E	*LN*	BN		82231	**VE**	E		WS
82215	**VE**	E	*LN*	BN						

DRIVING BRAKE VAN (110 mph)

Mark 3B. Air conditioned. T4 bogies. dg. ETS 6X.

82301–305 originally converted 2008. 82306–308 converted 2011–12. 82309 converted 2013.

g Fitted with a diesel generator for use while stabled in terminal stations or at depots. 48.5 t.

Lot No. 31042 Derby 1988. 45.2 t.

82301	(82117)	g	**CM**	AV	*CR*	AL
82302	(82151)	g	**CM**	AV	*CR*	AL
82303	(82135)	g	**CM**	AV	*CR*	AL
82304	(82130)	g	**CM**	AV	*CR*	AL
82305	(82134)	g	**CM**	AV	*CR*	AL
82306	(82144)		**AW**	AV	*TW*	CF
82307	(82131)		**AW**	AV	*TW*	CF
82308	(82108)		**AW**	AV	*TW*	CF
82309	(82104)	g	**CM**	AV	*CR*	AL

GANGWAYED BRAKE VAN (100 mph)

Mark 1. Short frame (57 ft). Load 10 t. Adapted 199? for use as Brake Luggage Van. Guard's compartment retained and former baggage area adapted for secure stowage of passengers' luggage. B4 bogies. 100 mph. ETS 1X.

Lot No. 30162 Pressed Steel 1956–57. 30.5 t.

92904 (80867, 99554)   **VN**   WC   *WC*   CS

HIGH SECURITY GENERAL UTILITY VAN

Mark 1. Short frame (57 ft). Load 14 t. Modified with new floors, three roller shutter doors per side and the end doors removed. Commonwealth bogies. ETS 0X.

Lot No. 30616 Pressed Steel 1959–60. 32 t.

94225 (86849, 93849)   **M**   WC   *WC*   CS

GENERAL UTILITY VAN (100 mph)

Mark 1. Short frame (57 ft). Load 14 t. Screw couplers. Adapted 2013/2010 for use as a water carrier with 3000 gallon capacity. ETS 0.

Non-standard livery: 96100 GWR Brown.

96100. Lot No. 30565 Pressed Steel 1959. 30 t. B5 bogies.
96175. Lot No. 30403 York/Glasgow 1958–60. 32 t. Commonwealth bogies.

96100 (86734, 93734)   x   **0**   VT   *VT*   TM
96175 (86628, 93628)   x   **M**   WC   *WC*   CS

KITCHEN CAR

Mark 1 converted from Corridor First in 2008 with staff accommodation. Commonwealth bogies. ETS 3.

Lot No. 30667 Swindon 1961. 35 t.

99316 (13321)   x   **M**   WC   *WC*   CS

BUFFET STANDARD

Mark 1 converted from Open Standard in 2013 by the removal of two seating bays and fitting of a buffet. –/48 2T. Commonwealth bogies. ETS 4.

Lot No. 30646 Wolverton 1961. 36 t.

99318 (4912)   x   **M**   WC   *WC*   CS

KITCHEN CAR

Mark 1 converted from Corridor Standard in 2011 with staff accommodation. Commonwealth bogies. ETS 3.

Lot No. 30685 Derby 1961–62. 34 t.

99712 (18893)	x	**M**	WC	*WC*	CS

OPEN STANDARD

Mark 1 Corridor Standard rebuilt in 1997 as Open Standard using components from 4936. –/64 2T. Commonwealth bogies. ETS 4.

Lot No. 30685 Derby 1961–62. 36 t.

99722 (25806, 18806)	x	**M**	WC	*WC*	CS

LUL 4 TC USED AS HAULED STOCK

The Class 438 4 TC sets were unpowered units designed to work in push-pull mode with Class 430 (4 Rep) tractor units and Class 33/1, 73 and 74 locomotives. They were converted from locomotive-hauled coaching stock built 1952–57.

The vehicles listed are owned by London Underground and used on both special services on the LU Metropolitan Line and on occasional specials on the National Rail network, top-and-tailed by locomotives.

Mark 1. Trailer Brake Second side corridor with Lavatory (TBSK). Lot No. 30229. Metro-Cammell 1957. 35.5 t.

70823 (34970)	**M**	LU	*WC*	RS

Mark 1. Trailer First side corridor with Lavatory (TFK). Lot No. 30019. Swindon 1954. 33.5 t.

71163 (13097)	**M**	LU	*WC*	RS

Mark 1. Driving Trailer Second Open (DTSO).

76297. Lot No. 30086. Eastleigh 1955. 32.0 t.
76324. Lot No. 30149. Swindon 1956. 32.0 t.

76297 (3938)	**M**	LU	*WC*	RS
76324 (4009)	**M**	LU	*WC*	RS

NNR REGISTERED CARRIAGES

These carriages are permitted to operate on the national railway network only between Sheringham and Cromer as an extension of North Norfolk Railway (NNR) "North Norfolkman" services. Only NNR coaches currently registered for use on the national railway network are listed.

KITCHEN BUFFET STANDARD

Mark 1. Built as Unclassified Restaurant. Rebuilt with Buffet Counter and seating reduced. –/23. Commonwealth bogies. Lot No. 30632 Swindon 1960–61. 39 t.

1969   v   **CC**   NN   *NY*   NO

OPEN FIRST

Mark 1. 42/–. Commonwealth bogies. Lot No. 30697 Swindon 1962–63. 36 t.

3116   v   **CC**   NN   *NY*   NO

OPEN STANDARD

Mark 1. –/48 2T. BR Mark 1 bogies. Lot No. 30121 Eastleigh 1953–55. 32 t.

4372   v   **CC**   NN   *NY*   NO

GANGWAYED BRAKE VAN

Mark 1. Short frame (57 ft). Now fitted with a kitchen. BR Mark 1 bogies. Lot No. 30224 Cravens 1955–56. 31.5 t.

81033   v   **CC**   NN   *NY*   NO

NYMR REGISTERED CARRIAGES

These carriages are permitted to operate on the national railway network but may only be used to convey fare-paying passengers between Middlesbrough and Whitby on the Esk Valley branch as an extension of North Yorkshire Moors Railway services between Pickering and Grosmont. Only NYMR coaches currently registered for use on the national railway network are listed.

RESTAURANT FIRST

Mark 1. 24/–. Commonwealth bogies. Lot No. 30633 Swindon 1961. 42.5 t.

324	x	**PC**	NY	*NY*		NY	JOS de CRAU

BUFFET STANDARD

Mark 1. –/44 2T. Commonwealth bogies.
Lot No. 30520 Wolverton 1960. 38 t.

1823	v	**M**	NY	*NY*		NY

OPEN STANDARD

Mark 1. –/64 2T (* –/60 2W 2T, † –/60 3W 1T). BR Mark 1 bogies.
3798/3801. Lot No. 30079 York 1953. 33 t.
3860/72. Lot No. 30080 York 1954. 33 t.
3948. Lot No. 30086 Eastleigh 1954–55. 33 t.
4198/4252. Lot No. 30172 York 1956. 33 t.
4286/90. Lot No. 30207 BRCW 1956. 33 t.
4455. Lot No. 30226 BRCW 1957. 33 t.

3798	v	**M**	NY	*NY*	NY		4198	v	**CC**	NY	*NY*	NY
3801	v	**CC**	NY	*NY*	NY		4252	v*	**CC**	NY	*NY*	NY
3860	v*	**M**	NY	*NY*	NY		4286	v	**CC**	NY	*NY*	NY
3872	v†	**BG**	NY	*NY*	NY		4290	v	**M**	NY	*NY*	NY
3948	v	**CC**	NY	*NY*	NY		4455	v	**CC**	NY	*NY*	NY

OPEN STANDARD

Mark 1. –/48 2T. BR Mark 1 bogies.
4786. Lot No. 30376 York 1957. 33 t.
4817. Lot No. 30473 BRCW 1959. 33 t.

4786	v	**CH**	NY	*NY*	NY		4817	v	**M**	NY	*NY*	NY

OPEN STANDARD

Mark 1. Later vehicles built with Commonwealth bogies. –/64 2T.
Lot No. 30690 Wolverton 1961–62. Aluminium window frames. 37 t.

4990	v	**M**	NY	*NY*	NY		5029	v	**CH**	NY	*NY*	NY
5000	v	**M**	NY	*NY*	NY							

OPEN BRAKE STANDARD

Mark 1. –/39 1T. BR Mark 1 bogies.
Lot No. 30170 Doncaster 1956. 34 t.

| 9225 | v | **M** | NY | *NY* | NY | | 9274 | v | **M** | NY | *NY* | NY |

CORRIDOR COMPOSITE

Mark 1. 24/18 1T. BR Mark 1 bogies.
15745. Lot No. 30179 Metro Cammell 1956. 36 t.
16156. Lot No. 30665 Derby 1961. 36 t.

| 15745 | v | **M** | NY | *NY* | NY | | 16156 | v | **CC** | NY | *NY* | NY |

CORRIDOR BRAKE COMPOSITE

Mark 1. Two First Class and three Standard Class compartments. 12/18 2T. BR Mark 1 bogies.
Lot No. 30185 Metro Cammell 1956. 36 t.

| 21100 | v | **CC** | NY | *NY* | NY |

CORRIDOR BRAKE STANDARD

Mark 1. –/24 1T. BR Mark 1 bogies.
Lot No. 30233 Gloucester 1957. 35 t.

| 35089 | v | **CC** | NY | *NY* | NY |

PULLMAN BRAKE THIRD

Built 1928 by Metropolitan Carriage & Wagon Company. –/30. Gresley bogies. 37.5 t.

| 232 | v | **PC** | NY | *NY* | NY | CAR No. 79 |

PULLMAN KITCHEN FIRST

Built by Metro-Cammell 1960–61 for East Coast Main Line services. 20/– 2T. Commonwealth bogies. 41.2 t.

| 318 | x | **PC** | NY | *NY* | NY | ROBIN |

PULLMAN PARLOUR FIRST

Built by Metro-Cammell 1960–61 for East Coast Main Line services. 29/– 2T. Commonwealth bogies. 38.5 t.

| 328 | x | **PC** | NY | *NY* | NY | OPAL |

2. HIGH SPEED TRAIN TRAILER CARS

HSTs consist of a number of trailer cars (usually between four and nine) with a power car at each end. All trailers are classified Mark 3 and have BT10 bogies with disc brakes and central door locking. Heating is by a 415 V three-phase supply and vehicles have air conditioning. Maximum speed is 125 mph.

The trailer cars have one standard 23 m bodyshell for both First and Standard Class, thus facilitating easy conversion from one class to the other. As built all cars had facing seating around tables with Standard Class carriages having nine bays of seats per side which did not line up with the eight windows per side.

All vehicles underwent a mid-life refurbishment in the 1980s with Standard Class seating layouts revised to incorporate unidirectional seating in addition to facing. A further refurbishment programme was completed in November 2000, with each company having a different scheme as follows:

Great Western Trains (later First Great Western). Green seat covers and extra partitions between seat bays.

Great North Eastern Railway. New lighting panels and brown seat covers.

Virgin CrossCountry. Green seat covers. Standard Class vehicles had four seats in the centre of each carriage replaced with a luggage stack. All have now passed to other operators.

Midland Mainline. Grey seat covers, redesigned seat squabs, side carpeting and two seats in the centre of each Standard Class carriage and one in First Class carriages replaced with a luggage stack.

Since then there have been many separate, and very different, refurbishment projects:

Midland Mainline was first to refurbish its vehicles a second time during 2003–04. This involved fitting new fluorescent and halogen ceiling lighting, although the original seats were retained in First and Standard Class, but with blue upholstery.

London St Pancras–Sheffield/Leeds and Nottingham services are now operated by **East Midlands Railway**. In previous operator East Midlands Trains embarked on another, less radical, refurbishment in 2009–10 which included retention of the original seats but with red upholstery in Standard Class and blue in First Class.

First Great Western (now **Great Western Railway**) started a major rebuild of its HST sets in late 2006, with the programme completed in 2008. The new interiors featured new lighting and seating throughout. First Class seats had leather upholstery, and were made by Primarius UK. Standard Class seats were of high-back design by Grammer. A number of sets operated without a full buffet or kitchen car, instead using one of 19 TS vehicles converted to include a "mini buffet" counter for use on shorter distance services. During 2012 15 402xx or 407xx buffet vehicles were converted to Trailer Standards to make the rakes formed as 7-cars up to 8-cars.

Great Western Railway is retaining 11 short 4-car sets for local and regional services. Trailers for these sets are being fitted with power doors and renumbered in the 48xxx and 49xxx series'.

Having increased its sets to 9-car sets in 2004, at the end of 2006 **GNER** embarked on a major rebuild of its HSTs. All vehicles have similar interiors to the Mark 4 "Mallard" fleet, with new Primarius seating. The refurbishment of the 13 sets was completed by **National Express East Coast** in late 2009, these trains were later operated by **Virgin Trains East Coast** and now **London North Eastern Railway**. VTEC refurbished its sets in 2015–16, with the same seats retained but with new upholstery, and leather in First Class.

Open access operator **Grand Central** started operation in December 2007 with a new service from Sunderland to London King's Cross. This operator had three sets mostly using stock converted from loco-hauled Mark 3s. The seats in Standard Class have First Class spacing and in most vehicles are all facing. These sets were withdrawn in December 2017 and transferred to East Midlands Trains (now EMR). They were refurbished in 2018–19, with ex-GWR buffet cars used instead of the original Grand Central buffet cars.

CrossCountry reintroduced HSTs to the Cross-Country network from 2008. Five sets were refurbished at Wabtec, Doncaster principally for use on the Plymouth–Edinburgh route. Three of these sets use stock mostly converted from loco-hauled Mark 3s and two are sets ex-Midland Mainline. The interiors are similar to refurbished East Coast sets, although the seating layout is different and one toilet per carriage has been removed in favour of a luggage stack. These sets are currently being fitted with sliding power doors.

ScotRail started operating HSTs from October 2018. The operator will use refurbished former GWR power cars and trailers (with sliding power doors) to form 17 5-car and nine 4-car sets for use between Glasgow/Edinburgh and Aberdeen/Inverness, as well as on the Aberdeen–Inverness route. Initially some unrefurbished sets are being used as cover whilst the heavily delayed programme to fit the 26 sets with sliding power doors is completed.

Operator Codes

Operator codes are shown in the heading before each set of vehicles. The first letter is always "T" for HST carriages, denoting a Trailer vehicle. The second letter denotes the passenger accommodation in that vehicle, for example "F" for First. "GS" denotes Guards accommodation and Standard Class seating. This is followed by catering provision, with "B" for buffet, and "K" for a kitchen and buffet:

TC	Trailer Composite		TGFB	Trailer Guard's Buffet First
TCK	Trailer Composite Kitchen		TSB	Trailer Buffet Standard
TF	Trailer First		TS	Trailer Standard
TFB	Trailer Buffet First		TGS	Trailer Guard's Standard
TFKB	Trailer Kitchen Buffet First			

Power doors: At the time of writing vehicles operated by CrossCountry, Great Western Railway and ScotRail are being fitted with power sliding doors and retention toilets. Those vehicles completed so far are shown with a "p" in the Notes column.

TRAILER BUFFET STANDARD   TSB

19 vehicles converted at Laira 2009–10 from HST TSs for First Great Western. Refurbished with Grammer seating.

40101–119. For Lot No. details see TS. –/70 1T. 35.5 t.

40101 (42170)	**FD**	P	LM
40102 (42223)	**FD**	P	LM
40103 (42316)	**GW**	P	LM
40104 (42254)	**FD**	P	LM
40105 (42084)	**FD**	P	LM
40106 (42162)	**FD**	P	LM
40107 (42334)	**FD**	P	LM
40108 (42314)	**GW**	P	LM
40109 (42262)	**FD**	P	LM
40110 (42187)	**FD**	P	LM
40111 (42248)	**FD**	P	LM
40112 (42336)	**FD**	P	LM
40113 (42309)	**GW**	P	LM
40114 (42086)	**FD**	P	LM
40115 (42320)	**FD**	P	LM
40116 (42147)	**FD**	P	LM
40117 (42249)	**GW**	P	LM
40118 (42338)	**FD**	P	LM
40119 (42090)	**FD**	P	LM

TRAILER BUFFET FIRST   TFB

Converted from TSB by fitting First Class seats. Renumbered from 404xx series by subtracting 200. All refurbished by First Great Western and fitted with Primarius leather seating. 23/–.

40204–221. Lot No. 30883 Derby 1976–77. 36.12 t.
40231. Lot No. 30899 Derby 1978–79. 36.12 t.

40204	**EA**	A	*EM*	DY	40210	**FD**	A		EP
40205	**EA**	A	*EM*	DY	40221	**EA**	A	*EM*	DY
40207	**FD**	A		ZH	40231	**FD**	A		EP

TRAILER BUFFET STANDARD   TSB

Renumbered from 400xx series by adding 400. –/33 1W.

40433 was numbered 40233 for a time when fitted with 23 First Class seats.

40402–426. Lot No. 30883 Derby 1976–77. 36.12 t.
40433. Lot No. 30899 Derby 1978–79. 36.12 t.

40402	**V**	AV	ZR	40426	**GC**	A		EP
40424	**GC**	A	DY	40433	**GC**	A		EP

TRAILER GUARD'S MINIATURE BUFFET FIRST   TGFB

Refurbished 2018–20 for ScotRail. Former Great Western Railway vehicles. Primarius leather seating. Fitted with a new corner buffet counter and kitchen. 32/– 1T.

40601–626. For Lot No. details see TF. 39.1 t.

40601	(41032)	p	SI	A	*SR*	IS		40614	(41010)		SI			
40602	(41038)	p	SI	A	*SR*	IS		40615	(41022)		SI			
40603	(41052)		SI					40616	(41142)	p	SI	A	*SR*	IS
40604	(41024)	p	SI	A	*SR*	IS		40617	(41144)		SI			
40605	(41094)	p	SI	A	*SR*	IS		40618	(41016)		SI			
40606	(41104)		SI					40619	(41124)		SI			
40607	(41136)		SI					40620	(41158)		SI			
40608	(41122)	p	SI	A	*SR*	IS		40621	(41146)		SI			
40609	(41020)		SI					40622	(41006)		SI			
40610	(41103)		SI					40623	(41180)		SI			
40611	(41130)		SI					40624	(41116)	p	SI	A	*SR*	IS
40612	(41134)	p	SI	A	*SR*	IS		40625	(41137)	p	SI	A	*SR*	IS
40613	(41135)		SI					40626	(41012)		SI			

TRAILER KITCHEN BUFFET FIRST   TFKB

These vehicles have larger kitchens than the 402xx and 404xx series vehicles, and are used in trains where a full meal service is required. They were renumbered from the 403xx series (in which the seats were unclassified) by adding 400 to the previous number. 17/–.

*   Refurbished Great Western Railway vehicles. Primarius leather seating.
m   Refurbished LNER vehicles with Primarius seating.

40700–721. Lot No. 30921 Derby 1978–79. 38.16 t.
40722–735. Lot No. 30940 Derby 1979–80. 38.16 t.
40737–753. Lot No. 30948 Derby 1980–81. 38.16 t.
40754–757. Lot No. 30966 Derby 1982. 38.16 t.

40700		ST	P	*EM*	NL		40721	*	FD	A		EP
40701	m	VE	P	*LN*	EC		40722	*	FD	A		EP
40702	m	VE	P	*LN*	EC		40727	*	FD	A		EP
40703	*	FD	A		ZB		40728		ST	P	*EM*	NL
40704	m	VE	A	*LN*	EC		40730		ST	P	*EM*	NL
40705	m	VE	A	*LN*	EC		40732		VE	P	*LN*	EC
40706	m	VE	A	*LN*	EC		40733	*	FD	A		EP
40707	*	FD	A		EP		40734	*	FD	A		EP
40708	m	VE	P	*LN*	EC		40735	m	VE	A	*LN*	EC
40710	*	FD	A		EP		40737	*	FD	A		EP
40711	m	VE	A	*LN*	EC		40739	*	FD	A		EP
40713	*	FD	A		EP		40740	m	VE	A	*LN*	EC
40715	*	GW	A		EP		40741		ST	P	*EM*	NL
40716	*	FD	A		EP		40742	m	VE	A	*LN*	EC
40718	*	FD	A		EP		40743	*	GW	A		EP
40720	m	VE	A	*LN*	EC		40746		ST	P	*EM*	NL

40748	m	**VE**	A	*LN*	EC	40753		**ST**	P	*EM*	NL
40749		**ST**	P	*EM*	NL	40754		**ST**	P	*EM*	NL
40750	m	**VE**	A	*LN*	EC	40755	*	**GW**	A		EP
40751		**VE**	P	*EM*	NL	40756		**ST**	P	*EM*	NL
40752	*	**FD**	A		EP	40757	*	**FD**	A		EP

TRAILER KITCHEN BUFFET FIRST   TFKB

These vehicles have been converted from TSBs in the 404xx series to be similar to the 407xx series vehicles. 17/–.

40802/804/811 were numbered 40212/232/211 for a time when fitted with 23 First Class seats.

*   Refurbished Great Western Railway vehicles. Primarius leather seating.
m   Refurbished LNER vehicle with Primarius seating.

40801–803/805/808/809/811. Lot No. 30883 Derby 1976–77. 38.16 t.
40804/806/807/810. Lot No. 30899 Derby 1978–79. 38.16 t.

40801	(40027, 40427)	*	**GW**	P		LM
40802	(40012, 40412)	*	**FD**	P		LM
40803	(40018, 40418)	*	**GW**	P		LM
40804	(40032, 40432)	*	**FD**	P		LM
40805	(40020, 40420)	m	**VE**	P	*LN*	EC
40806	(40029, 40429)	*	**FD**	P		LM
40807	(40035, 40435)	*	**FD**	P		LM
40808	(40015, 40415)	*	**FD**	P		LM
40809	(40014, 40414)	*	**FD**	P		LM
40810	(40030, 40430)	*	**FD**	P		LM
40811	(40011, 40411)	*	**FD**	P		LM

TRAILER BUFFET FIRST   TFB

Converted from TSB by First Great Western. Refurbished with Primarius leather seating. 23/–.

40900/902/904. Lot No. 30883 Derby 1976–77. 36.12 t.
40901/903. Lot No. 30899 Derby 1978–79. 36.12 t.

40900	(40022, 40422)	**FD**	FG	*HT*	PM
40901	(40036, 40436)	**GW**	P		LM
40902	(40023, 40423)	**FD**	FG	*HT*	PM
40903	(40037, 40437)	**GW**	P		LM
40904	(40001, 40401)	**GW**	FG	*HT*	PM

TRAILER FIRST   TF

As built and m 48/– 2T (m† 48/– 1T – one toilet removed for trolley space).
*   Refurbished Great Western Railway vehicles. Primarius leather seating.
c   Refurbished CrossCountry vehicles with Primarius seating and 2 tip-up seats. One toilet removed. 40/– 1TD 1W.
m   Refurbished LNER vehicles with Primarius seating.
px Refurbished CrossCountry vehicles with power doors, Primarius seating

and one toilet removed. 39/– 1TD 1W.
s   Fitted with centre luggage stack, disabled toilet and wheelchair space. 46/– 1T 1TD 1W.
w   Wheelchair space. 47/– 2T 1W. (41154 47/– 1TD 1T 1W).
x   Toilet removed for trolley space (FGW). 48/– 1T.

41004–056. Lot No. 30881 Derby 1976–77. 33.66 t.
41057–120. Lot No. 30896 Derby 1977–78. 33.66 t.
41122–146. Lot No. 30938 Derby 1979–80. 33.66 t.
41149–166. Lot No. 30947 Derby 1980. 33.66 t.
41167/169. Lot No. 30963 Derby 1982. 33.66 t.
41170. Lot No. 30967 Derby 1982. Former prototype vehicle. 33.66 t.
41176. Lot No. 30897 Derby 1977. 33.66 t.
41180. Lot No. 30884 Derby 1976–77. 33.66 t.
41182/183/189. Lot No. 30939 Derby 1979–80. 33.66 t.
41185–187. Lot No. 30969 Derby 1982. 33.66 t.
41190. Lot No. 30882 Derby 1976–77. 33.60 t.
41192. Lot No. 30897 Derby 1977–79. 33.60 t.

No.						No.					
41004	*x	**FD**	A		EP	41072	s	**ST**	P	*EM*	NL
41006	*w	**GW**	A		ZB	41075		**ST**	P	*EM*	NL
41008	*w	**FD**	A		EP	41076	s	**ST**	P	*EM*	NL
41010	*w	**FD**	A	*SR*	IS	41077		**ST**	P	*EM*	NL
41012	*w	**GW**	A		ZB	41079		**ST**	P	*EM*	NL
41016	*w	**FD**	A		ZB	41083	mw	**VE**	P	*LN*	EC
41018	*w	**FD**	A		EP	41084	s	**ST**	P	*EM*	NL
41020	*w	**FD**	A		ZB	41087	mt	**VE**	A	*LN*	EC
41022	*w	**FD**	A	*SR*	IS	41088	mw	**VE**	A	*LN*	EC
41026	px	**XC**	A	*XC*	LA	41089	*w	**FD**	A		EP
41028	*w	**FD**	A		EP	41090	mt	**VE**	A	*LN*	EC
41030	*w	**FD**	A		EP	41091	mt	**VE**	A	*LN*	EC
41034	*w	**FD**	A		EP	41092	mw	**VE**	A	*LN*	EC
41035	c	**XC**	A	*XC*	LA	41095	mw	**VE**	P	*LN*	EC
41039	mt	**VE**	A	*LN*	EC	41097	mt	**VE**	A	*LN*	EC
41040	mw	**VE**	A	*LN*	EC	41098	mw	**VE**	A	*LN*	EC
41041	s	**ST**	P	*EM*	NL	41099	mt	**VE**	A	*LN*	EC
41044	mw	**VE**	A	*LN*	EC	41100	mw	**VE**	A	*LN*	EC
41046	s	**ST**	P	*EM*	NL	41102	*w	**FD**	A		EP
41052	*w	**FD**	A		EP	41103	*x	**FD**	A		ZB
41056	*w	**FD**	A		EP	41104	*w	**FD**	A	*SR*	IS
41057		**ST**	P	*EM*	NL	41106	*w	**FD**	A		EP
41059	*w	**GW**	FG		LM	41108	*w	**GW**	P		LM
41061	w	**ST**	P	*EM*	NL	41110	*w	**FD**	A		EP
41062		**VE**	P	*LN*	EC	41111		**ST**	P	*EM*	NL
41063		**ST**	P	*EM*	NL	41112		**VE**	P	*LN*	NL
41064	s	**ST**	P	*EM*	NL	41113	s	**ST**	P	*EM*	NL
41066	mt	**VE**	A	*LN*	EC	41115	mt	**VE**	P	*LN*	EC
41067	s	**ST**	P	*EM*	NL	41117		**ST**	P	*EM*	NL
41068	w	**VE**	P	*LN*	NL	41118	mw	**VE**	A	*LN*	EC
41069	s	**ST**	P	*EM*	NL	41120	mt	**VE**	A	*LN*	EC
41070	s	**ST**	P	*EM*	NL	41124	*w	**FD**	A	*SR*	IS
41071		**ST**	P	*EM*	NL	41126	*w	**FD**	A	*SR*	IS

41128	*w	**FD**	A		EP
41130	*w	**FD**	A	*SR*	IS
41132	*w	**FD**	A		EP
41135	*w	**FD**	A	*SR*	IS
41136	*w	**FD**	A	*SR*	IS
41138	*w	**FD**	A		EP
41140	*w	**FD**	A	*SR*	IS
41144	*w	**FD**	A	*SR*	IS
41146	*w	**GW**	A		ZB
41149	*w	**GW**	P		LM
41150	mw	**VE**	A	*LN*	EC
41151	mt	**VE**	A	*LN*	EC
41152	mw	**VE**	A	*LN*	EC
41154	w	**VE**	P	*LN*	EC
41156		**ST**	P	*EM*	NL
41158	*w	**GW**	A	*SR*	IS
41159	mt	**VE**	P	*LN*	EC
41160	*w	**GW**	FG	*HT*	PM
41161	*w	**GW**	P		LM
41162	*w	**GW**	P		LM
41164	mw	**VE**	A	*LN*	EC
41165	mw	**VE**	P	*LN*	EC
41166	*w	**GW**	FG	*HT*	PM
41167	*w	**FD**	FG	*HT*	PM
41169	*w	**FD**	P		LM

41193–195/201–206. Lot No. 30878 Derby 1975–76. 34.3 t. Converted from Mark 3A Open First.
41207–209. Lot No. 30877 Derby 1975–77. Converted from Mark 3A Open Standard.

41170	(41001)	mt	**VE**	A	*LN*	EC
41176	(42142, 42352)	*w	**GW**	P		LM
41180	(40511)	*w	**FD**	A		ZB
41182	(42278)	*w	**GW**	P		LM
41183	(42274)	*w	**GW**	P		LM
41185	(42313)	mt	**VE**	P	*LN*	EC
41186	(42312)	*w	**FD**	P		LM
41187	(42311)	*w	**FD**	P		LM
41189	(42298)	*w	**GW**	P		LM
41190	(42088)	mt	**VE**	P	*LN*	EC
41192	(42246)	*w	**GW**	P		LM

The following carriages have been converted from loco-hauled Mark 3 vehicles.

41193	(11060)	px	**XC**	P	*XC*	LA
41194	(11016)	c	**XC**	P	*XC*	LA
41195	(11020)	px	**XC**	P	*XC*	LA
41204	(11023)		**EA**	A	*EM*	DY
41205	(11036)	w	**EA**	A	*EM*	DY
41206	(11055)		**EA**	A	*EM*	DY
41207	(12033, 42403)		**EA**	A	*EM*	DY
41208	(12112, 42406)	w	**EA**	A	*EM*	DY
41209	(12088, 42409)		**EA**	A	*EM*	DY

TRAILER STANDARD   TS

42158 was numbered 41177 for a time when fitted with First Class seats.
42310 was numbered 41188 for a time when fitted with First Class seats.

Standard seating and m –/76 2T.
* Refurbished Great Western Railway vehicles. Grammer seating. –/80 2T. (unless h – high density).
c Refurbished CrossCountry vehicles with Primarius seating. –/82 1T.
§c Refurbished CrossCountry vehicles with Primarius seating and 2 tip-up

seats. –/66 1TD 2W. 42379/380 are –/71 1TD 1T 2W.
d Great Western Railway vehicles with universal access toilet and 5, 6 or 7 tip-up seats. –/68 1T 1TD 2W.
h "High density" Great Western Railway vehicles. –/84 2T.
k "High density" Great Western Railway refurbished vehicle with disabled persons toilet and 5, 6 or 7 tip-up seats. –/72 1T 1TD 2W.
m Refurbished LNER vehicles with Primarius seating.
pr Refurbished ScotRail vehicles with power doors and Grammer seating. –/74.
ps Refurbished ScotRail vehicles with power doors and Grammer seating. –/74 1T.
p* Refurbished ScotRail vehicles with power doors, Grammer seating and universal access toilet. –/58 1TD 2W.
px Refurbished CrossCountry vehicles with power doors and Primarius seating. –/80 1T.
pt Refurbished CrossCountry vehicles with power doors, Primarius seating and universal access toilet. –/64 1TD 2W.
u Centre luggage stack (EMR) –/74 2T.
w Centre luggage stack and wheelchair space (EMR) –72 2T 1W.
† Disabled persons toilet (LNER) –/62 1T 1TD 1W.

42003–089/362. Lot No. 30882 Derby 1976–77. 33.6 t.
42091–250. Lot No. 30897 Derby 1977–79. 33.6 t.
42251–305. Lot No. 30939 Derby 1979–80. 33.6 t.
42306–322. Lot No. 30969 Derby 1982. 33.6 t.
42323–341. Lot No. 30983 Derby 1984–85. 33.6 t.
42342/360. Lot No. 30949 Derby 1982. 33.47 t. Converted from TGS.
42343/345. Lot No. 30970 Derby 1982. 33.47 t. Converted from TGS.
42344/361. Lot No. 30964 Derby 1982. 33.47 t. Converted from TGS.
42346/347/350/351/379/380/551–564. Lot No. 30881 Derby 1976–77. 33.66 t. Converted from TF.
42348/349/363/364/381/565–570. Lot No. 30896 Derby 1977–78. 33.66 t. Converted from TF.
42354. Lot No. 30897 Derby 1977. Was TF from 1983 to 1992. 33.66 t.
42353/355–357. Lot No. 30967 Derby 1982. Ex-prototype vehicles. 33.66 t.
42366–378/382/383/401–409. Lot No. 30877 Derby 1975–77. 34.3 t. Converted from Mark 3A Open Standard.
42384. Lot No. 30896 Derby 1977–78. 33.66 t. Converted from TF.
42501/509/513/515/517. Lot No. 30948 Derby 1980–81. 34.8 t. Converted from TFKB.
42502/506/508/514/516. Lot No. 30940 Derby 1979–80. 34.8 t. Converted from TFKB.
42503/504/510/511. Lot No. 30921 Derby 1978–79. 34.8 t. Converted from TFKB.
42505/507/512/518/519. Lot No. 30883 Derby 1976–77. 34.8 t. Converted from TSB.
42520. Lot No. 30899 Derby 1978–79. 34.8 t. Converted from TSB.
42571–579. Lot No. 30938 Derby 1979–80. 33.66 t. Converted from TF.
42580–583. Lot No. 30947 Derby 1980. 33.66 t. Converted from TF.
42584–586. Lot No. 30878 Derby 1975–76. Converted from Mark 3A Open First.

42003	*h	**FD**	A		ZB	**42007**	*d	**FD**	A		ZB
42004	p*	**SI**	A	*SR*	IS	**42008**	*k	**GW**	A		ZB
42005	*h	**GW**	A	*GW*	LA	**42009**	*h	**FD**	A		EP
42006	*h	**FD**	A		EP	**42010**	*h	**FD**	A	*SR*	IS

No.					
42012	*k	FD	A	SR	IS
42013	*h	FD	A	SR	IS
42014	*h	FD	A		ZB
42015	*k	GW	A	GW	LA
42016	*h	GW	A	GW	LA
42019	ps	SI	A	SR	IS
42021	*k	FD	A		ZB
42023	*h	FD	A		EP
42024	*k	FD	A	HT	PM
42025	*h	FD	A		EP
42026	*h	FD	A	HT	PM
42028	*h	FD	A		EP
42029	*h	FD	A		EP
42030	*k	FD	A	SR	IS
42031	*h	FD	A		EP
42032	*h	FD	A	SR	IS
42033	*	FD	A		ZB
42034	pr	SI	A	SR	IS
42035	*	FD	A		ZB
42036	px	XC	A	XC	LA
42037	c	XC	A	XC	LA
42038	c	XC	A	XC	LA
42039	*h	FD	A		EP
42040	*h	FD	A		EP
42041	*h	FD	A		EP
42042	*h	FD	A		ZB
42043	*h	FD	A		EP
42044	*h	FD	A		ZB
42045	ps	SI	A	SR	IS
42046	ps	SI	A	SR	IS
42047	*	FD	A	SR	IS
42048	*h	FD	A		EP
42049	*h	FD	A		EP
42050	*h	FD	A		EP
42051	px	XC	A	XC	LA
42052	c	XC	A	XC	LA
42053	c	XC	A	XC	LA
42054	*	FD	A		EP
42055	p*	SI	A	SR	IS
42056	*	FD	A		EP
42057	m	VE	A	LN	EC
42058	m	VE	A	LN	EC
42059	m	VE	A	LN	EC
42060	*h	FD	A		EP
42061	*h	FD	A		EP
42062	*k	FD	A		EP
42063	m	VE	A	LN	EC
42064	m	VE	A	LN	EC
42065	m	VE	A	LN	EC
42066	*k	FD	A		EP
42067	*h	FD	A		EP
42068	*h	FD	A		EP
42069	*k	FD	A	SR	IS
42070	*h	FD	A		EP
42071	*h	FD	A		EP
42072	*	FD	A		ZB
42074	*h	FD	A		EP
42075	ps	SI	A	SR	IS
42076	*	FD	A	SR	IS
42077	*	FD	A		EP
42078	*	FD	A		EP
42079	*h	FD	A		EP
42080	*h	FD	A		EP
42081	*k	FD	A		EP
42083	*h	FD	A		EP
42087	*h	GW	P	GW	LA
42089	*h	FD	A		EP
42091	m†	VE	A	LN	EC
42092	*k	FD	P	GW	LA
42094	*h	FD	FG	GW	LA
42095	*	FD	FG	GW	LA
42096	*h	FD	A		EP
42097	px	XC	A	XC	LA
42098	*h	FD	A		EP
42099	*h	FD	A		EP
42100	u	ST	P	EM	NL
42103	*k	FD	P	GW	LA
42104	m	VE	A	LN	EC
42105	*h	FD	P	GW	LA
42106	m	VE	A	LN	EC
42107	*	FD	A		ZB
42108	*h	FD	P		LM
42109	m	VE	A	LN	EC
42110	m	VE	A	LN	EC
42111	u	ST	P	EM	NL
42112	u	ST	P	EM	NL
42113	u	ST	P	EM	NL
42115	*h	FD	P		LM
42116	m†	VE	A	LN	EC
42117	m	VE	A	LN	EC
42118	*h	FD	A	SR	IS
42119	u	ST	P	EM	NL
42120	u	ST	P	EM	NL
42121	u	ST	P	EM	NL
42122	m	VE	A	LN	EC
42123		VE	P	LN	EC
42124	u	ST	P	EM	NL
42125		VE	P	LN	EC
42126	*h	FD	A		EP
42127	m†	VE	A	LN	EC
42128	m†	VE	A	LN	EC
42129	*	GW	A	SR	IS

42130	m	VE	P	LN	EC
42131	u	ST	P	EM	NL
42132	w	ST	P	EM	NL
42133	u	ST	P	EM	NL
42134	m	VE	A	LN	EC
42135	u	ST	P	EM	NL
42136	u	ST	P	EM	NL
42137	u	ST	P	EM	NL
42138	*k	FD	A		ZB
42139	u	ST	P	EM	NL
42140	u	ST	P	EM	NL
42141	u	ST	P	EM	NL
42143	*	FD	A		ZK
42144	*	FD	A		EP
42145	*	FD	A		ZK
42146	m	VE	A	LN	EC
42148	u	ST	P	EM	NL
42149	u	ST	P	EM	NL
42150	m	VE	A	LN	EC
42151	w	ST	P	EM	NL
42152	u	ST	P	EM	NL
42153	u	ST	P	EM	NL
42154	m	VE	A	LN	EC
42155	w	ST	P	EM	NL
42156	u	ST	P	EM	NL
42157	u	ST	P	EM	NL
42158	m	VE	A	LN	EC
42159	mt	VE	P	LN	EC
42160	m	VE	P	LN	EC
42161	mt	VE	P	LN	EC
42163	m	VE	P	LN	EC
42164		ST	P	EM	NL
42165		ST	P	EM	NL
42166	*h	FD	P		LM
42167	*h	FD	FG	GW	LA
42169	*h	FD	P		LM
42171	m	VE	A	LN	EC
42172	m	VE	A	LN	EC
42173	*k	FD	P		LM
42175	*h	FD	FG	GW	LA
42176	*h	GW	P	GW	LA
42178	*h	FD	P		LM
42179	m	VE	A	LN	EC
42180	m	VE	A	LN	EC
42181	m	VE	A	LN	EC
42182	m	VE	A	LN	EC
42183	p*	SI	A	SR	IS
42184	ps	SI	A	SR	IS
42185	*	FD	A		EP
42186	m	VE	A	LN	EC
42188	mt	VE	A	LN	EC
42189	mt	VE	A	LN	EC
42190	m	VE	A	LN	EC
42191	m	VE	A	LN	EC
42192	m	VE	A	LN	EC
42193	m	VE	A	LN	EC
42194	u	VE	P	LN	NL
42195	*k	FD	P		LM
42196	*h	FD	A		EP
42197	*h	FD	A		EP
42198	m	VE	A	LN	EC
42199	m	VE	A	LN	EC
42200	*d	GW	A	SR	IS
42202	*k	FD	A		ZB
42203	*h	FD	A		ZB
42205		VE	P	LN	EC
42206	*d	FD	A	SR	IS
42207	*d	FD	A	SR	IS
42208	*	FD	A	SR	IS
42209	*	FD	A	SR	IS
42210		VE	P	LN	EC
42211	*k	FD	A		ZB
42212	*h	FD	A		ZB
42213	*h	FD	A		EP
42214	*h	FD	A		ZB
42215	m	VE	A	LN	EC
42216	*h	FD	A		EP
42217	*k	FD	P		LM
42219	m	VE	A	LN	EC
42220	w	ST	P	EM	NL
42221	*h	FD	A		EP
42225		VE	P	LN	NL
42226	m	VE	A	LN	EC
42227		VE	P	LN	NL
42228	m	VE	P	LN	EC
42229		VE	P	LN	NL
42230	u	ST	P	EM	NL
42231	*h	FD	FG	GW	LA
42232	*h	GW	P		LM
42233	*h	FD	P		LM
42234	c	XC	P	XC	LA
42235	m	VE	A	LN	EC
42236	*h	FD	A		EP
42237	m	VE	P	LN	EC
42238	mt	VE	A	LN	EC
42239	mt	VE	A	LN	EC
42240	m	VE	A	LN	EC
42241	m	VE	A	LN	EC
42242	m	VE	A	LN	EC
42243	m	VE	A	LN	EC
42244	m	VE	A	LN	EC
42245	*	GW	A		ZN

42247	*h	**FD**	P		LM	42294	*	**FD**	P		LM
42250	*	**GW**	A		ZN	42295	*d	**FD**	A	*SR*	IS
42251	*k	**FD**	A		ZB	42296	*	**FD**	A		EP
42252	*	**FD**	A		ZB	42297	*	**FD**	A		ZB
42253	*	**FD**	A		ZB	42299	*d	**GW**	A		ZB
42255	*d	**FD**	A	*SR*	IS	42300	*	**GW**	A		ZB
42256	*	**FD**	A	*SR*	IS	42301	*	**GW**	A	*SR*	IS
42257	*	**FD**	A		ZB	42302	*k	**FD**	P	*GW*	LA
42259	p*	**SI**	A	*SR*	IS	42303	*h	**FD**	P		LM
42260	*h	**FD**	A		EP	42304	*h	**FD**	FG	*GW*	LA
42261	*h	**FD**	A	*SR*	IS	42305	*h	**GW**	P		LM
42263	*	**FD**	A		ZK	42306	m	**VE**	P	*LN*	EC
42264	*k	**FD**	A		ZB	42307	m	**VE**	P	*LN*	EC
42265	p*	**SI**	A	*SR*	IS	42308	*h	**FD**	P		LM
42267	*d	**FD**	A	*SR*	IS	42310	*k	**FD**	P	*GW*	LA
42268	*d	**FD**	A		ZB	42319	m	**GW**	P		LM
42269	*	**FD**	A	*SR*	IS	42321	*h	**FD**	P		LM
42272	*h	**FD**	A		EP	42322	m	**VE**	P	*LN*	EC
42275	p*	**SI**	A	*SR*	IS	42323	m	**VE**	A	*LN*	EC
42276	ps	**SI**	A	*SR*	IS	42325	*	**FD**	A	*SR*	IS
42277	*	**FD**	A		ZB	42326	m	**VE**	P	*LN*	EC
42279	*d	**FD**	A	*SR*	IS	42327	w	**ST**	P	*EM*	NL
42280	*	**FD**	A	*SR*	IS	42328	w	**ST**	P	*EM*	NL
42281	*	**FD**	A		ZB	42329	w	**ST**	P	*EM*	NL
42283	*h	**FD**	A		EP	42330	m	**VE**	P	*LN*	EC
42284	*h	**FD**	A		EP	42331	u	**ST**	P	*EM*	NL
42286	mt	**VE**	P	*LN*	EC	42332	*	**FD**	A		EP
42287	*k	**FD**	A	*SR*	IS	42333	ps	**SI**	A	*SR*	IS
42288	*h	**FD**	A		ZH	42335	w	**VE**	P	*LN*	EC
42289	*h	**FD**	A	*SR*	IS	42337	w	**ST**	P	*EM*	NL
42290	c	**XC**	P	*XC*	LA	42339	w	**ST**	P	*EM*	NL
42291	p*	**SI**	A	*SR*	IS	42340	m	**VE**	A	*LN*	EC
42292	p*	**SI**	A	*SR*	IS	42341	u	**ST**	P	*EM*	NL
42293	ps	**SI**	A	*SR*	IS						

42342	(44082)	px	**XC**	A	*XC*	LA
42343	(44095)	ps	**SI**	A	*SR*	IS
42344	(44092)	*k	**FD**	A	*SR*	IS
42345	(44096)	p*	**SI**	A	*SR*	IS
42346	(41053)	*h	**FD**	A		EP
42347	(41054)	*k	**FD**	A	*HT*	PM
42348	(41073)	*k	**FD**	A		EP
42349	(41074)	*h	**FD**	A		ZB
42350	(41047)	*	**FD**	A		ZB
42351	(41048)	*	**GW**	A		EP
42353	(42001, 41171)	*k	**FD**	P		LM
42354	(42114, 41175)	m	**VE**	A	*LN*	EC
42355	(42000, 41172)	m	**VE**	A	*LN*	EC
42356	(42002, 41173)	*k	**GW**	A		EP
42357	(41002, 41174)	m	**VE**	A	*LN*	EC
42360	(44084, 45084)	*h	**FD**	A		ZB
42361	(44099, 42000)	*h	**GW**	A		EP

42362	(42011, 41178)	*h	**FD**	A		EP
42363	(41082)	mt	**VE**	A	*LN*	EC
42364	(41080)	*k	**GW**	P	*GW*	LA

42366–378 were converted from loco-hauled Mark 3 vehicles for CrossCountry and 42382/383 for First Great Western.

42366	(12007)	pt	**XC**	P	*XC*	LA
42367	(12025)	c	**XC**	P	*XC*	LA
42368	(12028)	c	**XC**	P	*XC*	LA
42369	(12050)	px	**XC**	P	*XC*	LA
42370	(12086)	px	**XC**	P	*XC*	LA
42371	(12052)	§c	**XC**	P	*XC*	LA
42372	(12055)	c	**XC**	P	*XC*	LA
42373	(12071)	c	**XC**	P	*XC*	LA
42374	(12075)	pt	**XC**	P	*XC*	LA
42375	(12113)	px	**XC**	P	*XC*	LA
42376	(12085)	pt	**XC**	P	*XC*	LA
42377	(12102)	px	**XC**	P	*XC*	LA
42378	(12123)	px	**XC**	P	*XC*	LA
42379	(41036)	§c	**XC**	A	*XC*	LA
42380	(41025)	§c	**XC**	A	*XC*	LA
42381	(41058)	*k	**FD**	P		LM
42382	(12128)	*h	**GW**	P		LM
42383	(12172)	*h	**GW**	P		LM
42384	(41078)	w	**ST**	P	*EM*	NL

These carriages were converted from loco-hauled Mark 3 vehicles for Grand Central, now operated by East Midlands Railway. They have a lower density seating layout (most seats arranged around tables). –/62 2T.

42401	(12149)	**EA**	A	*EM*	DY
42402	(12155)	**EA**	A	*EM*	DY
42404	(12152)	**EA**	A	*EM*	DY
42405	(12136)	**EA**	A	*EM*	DY
42407	(12044)	**EA**	A	*EM*	DY
42408	(12121)	**EA**	A	*EM*	DY

These carriages have been converted from TFKB or TSB buffet cars to TS vehicles in 2011–12 (42501–515) and 2013–14 (42516–520) at Wabtec Kilmarnock for FGW. Refurbished with Grammer seating. –/84 1T. 34.8 t.

42501	(40344, 40744)	**FD**	A		EP
42502	(40331, 40731)	**FD**	A		ZB
42503	(40312, 40712)	**FD**	A		EP
42504	(40314, 40714)	**FD**	A		EP
42505	(40428, 40228)	**FD**	A		EP
42506	(40324, 40724)	**FD**	A	*HT*	PM
42507	(40409, 40209)	**FD**	A		EP
42508	(40325, 40725)	**FD**	A		EP
42509	(40336, 40736)	**GW**	A		EP
42510	(40317, 40717)	**FD**	A		EP
42511	(40309, 40709)	**FD**	A		EP
42512	(40408, 40208)	**GW**	A		EP

42513	(40338, 40738)		**FD**	A		EP
42514	(40326, 40726)		**FD**	A		EP
42515	(40347, 40747)		**FD**	A		EP
42516	(40323, 40723)		**FD**	A		EP
42517	(40345, 40745)		**FD**	A		EP
42518	(40003, 40403)		**FD**	P		LM
42519	(40016, 40416)		**FD**	P		LM
42520	(40234, 40434)		**FD**	P		LM

These carriages have been converted from TF to TS vehicles in 2014 at Wabtec Kilmarnock for FGW. Refurbished with Grammer seating. –/80 1T (pr –/74). 35.5 t.

42551	(41003)		**FD**	A		ZB
42552	(41007)		**FD**	A		EP
42553	(41009)	pr	**SI**	A	*SR*	IS
42554	(41011)		**GW**	A	*GW*	LA
42555	(41015)		**FD**	A		ZB
42556	(41017)		**FD**	A		EP
42557	(41019)		**FD**	A		ZB
42558	(41021)		**FD**	A		ZB
42559	(41023)	pr	**SI**	A	*SR*	IS
42560	(41027)		**FD**	A		EP
42561	(41031)	pr	**SI**	A	*SR*	IS
42562	(41037)	pr	**SI**	A	*SR*	IS
42563	(41045)		**FD**	FG	*GW*	LA
42564	(41051)		**FD**	A		EP
42565	(41085)		**FD**	FG	*GW*	LA
42566	(41086)		**FD**	FG	*GW*	LA
42567	(41093)		**FD**	A		ZB
42568	(41101)		**FD**	A		EP
42569	(41105)		**FD**	A		EP
42570	(41114)		**FD**	FG	*GW*	LA
42571	(41121)	pr	**SI**	A	*SR*	IS
42572	(41123)		**FD**	A	*SR*	IS
42573	(41127)		**FD**	A		EP
42574	(41129)		**FD**	A		ZB
42575	(41131)		**FD**	A		EP
42576	(41133)	pr	**SI**	A	*SR*	IS
42577	(41141)	pr	**SI**	A	*SR*	IS
42578	(41143)	pr	**SI**	A	*SR*	IS
42579	(41145)		**GW**	A	*SR*	IS
42580	(41155)		**FD**	P	*GW*	LA
42581	(41157)		**GW**	A		EP
42582	(41163)		**FD**	FG	*GW*	LA
42583	(41153, 42385)		**GW**	P		LM

These carriages were converted from loco-hauled carriages for Grand Central but have now been converted to TS for East Midlands Railway. –/62 2T.

42584	(11045, 41201)		**EA**	A	*EM*	DY
42585	(11017, 41202)		**EA**	A	*EM*	DY
42586	(11038, 41203)		**EA**	A	*EM*	DY

TRAILER GUARD'S STANDARD   TGS

As built and m –/65 1T.
* Refurbished Great Western Railway vehicles. Grammer seating and toilet removed for trolley store. –/67 (unless h).
c Refurbished CrossCountry vehicles with Primarius seating. –/67 1T.
p Refurbished CrossCountry vehicles with power doors and Primarius seating. –/67.
h "High density" Great Western Railway vehicles. –/71.
m Refurbished LNER vehicles with Primarius seating.
s Fitted with centre luggage stack (EMR) –/63 1T. 44027 is –/64 1T.
t Fitted with centre luggage stack –/61 1T.

44001–090. Lot No. 30949 Derby 1980–82. 33.47 t.
44091–094. Lot No. 30964 Derby 1982. 33.47 t.
44098–100. Lot No. 30970 Derby 1982. 33.47 t.

No.	mark	op	A/P	code	fin		No.	mark	op	A/P	code	fin
44001	*	FD	A		EP		44037	*h	FD	A	SR	IS
44002	*h	FD	A	HT	PM		44038	*	FD	A		EP
44003	*h	FD	A		ZB		44039	*	FD	A	SR	IS
44004	*h	FD	A	SR	IS		44040	*	GW	A		ZB
44005	*h	GW	A	GW	LA		44041	s	ST	P	EM	NL
44007	*h	FD	A		EP		44042	*h	FD	P	GW	LA
44008	*h	FD	A		ZB		44043	*h	FD	A		EP
44009	*h	FD	A		EP		44044	s	ST	P	EM	NL
44010	*h	FD	A	SR	IS		44045	m	VE	A	LN	EC
44011	*	FD	A		EP		44046	s	ST	P	EM	NL
44012	p	XC	A	XC	LA		44047	s	ST	P	EM	NL
44013	*h	FD	A		EP		44048	s	ST	P	EM	NL
44014	*h	FD	A		ZB		44049	*	FD	A		EP
44015	*	FD	A	SR	IS		44050	m	VE	P	LN	EC
44016	*h	FD	A		EP		44051	s	ST	P	EM	NL
44017	c	XC	A	XC	LA		44052	p	XC	P	XC	LA
44018	*	FD	A		EP		44054	s	ST	P	EM	NL
44019	m	VE	A	LN	EC		44056	m	VE	A	LN	EC
44020	*h	FD	A		EP		44057	m	VE	P	LN	EC
44021	p	XC	P	XC	LA		44058	m	VE	A	LN	EC
44022	*h	FD	A		EP		44059	*	FD	A		EP
44023	*h	FD	A	SR	IS		44060	*h	FD	P		LM
44024	*h	FD	A		EP		44061	m	VE	A	LN	EC
44025	*	FD	A		EP		44063	m	VE	A	LN	EC
44026	*h	FD	A		LA		44066	*	FD	A	SR	IS
44027	s	VE	P	LN	NL		44067	*h	FD	A		ZB
44028	*	FD	A		EP		44068	*h	FD	P	GW	LA
44029	*	FD	A	SR	IS		44069	*h	FD	P	GW	LA
44030	*h	FD	A	SR	IS		44070	s	ST	P	EM	NL
44031	m	VE	A	LN	EC		44071	s	ST	P	EM	NL
44032	*	FD	A	SR	IS		44072	c	XC	P	XC	LA
44034	*	FD	A	HT	PM		44073	†	VE	P	LN	EC
44035	*	FD	A	SR	IS		44074	*h	FD	P		LM
44036	*h	FD	A		ZB		44075	m	VE	P	LN	EC

44076	*h	FD	P	GW	LA
44077	m	VE	A	LN	EC
44078	*h	FD	P		LM
44080	m	VE	A	LN	EC
44081	*h	FD	P	GW	LA
44085	s	ST	P	EM	NL
44086	*	GW	A	SR	IS

44089	t	V	AV		ZR
44091	*h	FD	P		LM
44093	*h	FD	A		EP
44094	m	VE	A	LN	EC
44098	m	VE	A	LN	EC
44100	*h	FD	P	GW	LA

TRAILER COMPOSITE KITCHEN   TCK

Converted from Mark 3A Open Standard. Refurbished CrossCountry vehicles with Primarius seating. Small kitchen for the preparation of hot food and stowage space for two trolleys between First and Standard Class. One toilet removed. 30/10 1T.

p Fitted with power doors. 30/8 1T.

45001–005. Lot No. 30877 Derby 1975–77. 34.3 t.

45001	(12004)		XC	P	XC	LA
45002	(12106)		XC	P	XC	LA
45003	(12076)	p	XC	P	XC	LA
45004	(12077)	p	XC	P	XC	LA
45005	(12080)		XC	P	XC	LA

TRAILER COMPOSITE   TC

Converted from TF for First Great Western 2014–15. Refurbished with Grammer seating. 24/39 1T.

46001–004. Lot No. 30881 Derby 1976–77. 35.6 t. Converted from TF.
46005–009. Lot No. 30896 Derby 1977–78. 35.6 t. Converted from TF.
46010–013. Lot No. 30938 Derby 1979–80. 35.6 t. Converted from TF.
46014. Lot No. 30963 Derby 1982. 35.6 t. Converted from TF.
46015. Lot No. 30884 Derby 1976–77. 35.6 t. Converted from TF.
46016/017. Lot No. 30939 Derby 1979–80. 35.6 t. Converted from TF.
46018. Lot No. 30969 Derby 1982. 35.6 t. Converted from TF.

46001	(41005)	FD	A		EP
46002	(41029)	FD	A		EP
46003	(41033)	FD	A		EP
46004	(41055)	FD	A		EP
46005	(41065)	FD	A		EP
46006	(41081)	FD	P		LM
46007	(41096)	FD	P		LM
46008	(41109)	FD	P		LM
46009	(41119)	FD	P		LM
46010	(41125)	FD	A	SR	IS
46011	(41139)	FD	A		EP
46012	(41147)	FD	P		LM
46013	(41148)	FD	P		LM
46014	(41168)	FD	P		LM
46015	(40505, 41179)	FD	A		EP

46016	(42282, 41181)	**FD** P	LM
46017	(42270, 41184)	**FD** P	LM
46018	(42318, 41191)	**FD** P	LM

TRAILER STANDARD   TS

Refurbished for Great Western Railway 2017–19 and fitted with power doors and retention toilets. For use in 4-car sets on local and regional services across the South-West. –/84 1T († –/62 and 5 tip-ups 1TD 2W).

48101–135. For Lot No. details see TS. 36.3 t.

48101	(42093, 48111)	p	**GW**	FG	*GW*	LA
48102	(42218)	p†	**GW**	FG	*GW*	LA
48103	(42168, 48101)	p	**GW**	FG	*GW*	LA
48104	(41107, 42365)	p	**GW**	FG	*GW*	LA
48105	(42266)	p†	**GW**	FG	*GW*	LA
48106	(42258)	p	**GW**	FG	*GW*	LA
48107	(42101)	p	**GW**	FG	*GW*	LA
48108	(42174)	p†	**GW**	FG	*GW*	LA
48109	(42085)	p	**GW**	FG	*GW*	LA
48110	(42315)	p	**GW**	FG	*GW*	LA
48111	(42224)	p†	**GW**	FG	*GW*	LA
48112	(42222)	p	**GW**	FG	*GW*	LA
48113	(42177, 48102)	p	**GW**	FG	*GW*	LA
48114	(42317)	p†	**GW**	FG	*GW*	LA
48115	(42285)	p	**GW**	A	*GW*	LA
48116	(42273)	p	**GW**	A	*GW*	LA
48117	(42271)	p†	**GW**	A	*GW*	LA
48118	(42073)	p	**GW**	A	*GW*	LA
48119	(42204)	p	**GW**	A	*GW*	LA
48120	(42201)	p†	**GW**	A	*GW*	LA
48121	(42027)	p	**GW**	A	*GW*	LA
48122						
48123						
48124						
48125						
48126						
48127						
48128						
48129						
48130						
48131	(42102)	p	**GW**	FG	*GW*	LA
48132						
48133						
48134						
48135						

TRAILER GUARD'S STANDARD   TGS

Refurbished for Great Western Railway 2017–19 and fitted with power doors. –/71.

49101–113. For Lot No. details see TGS. 35.7 t.

49101	(44055)	p **GW**	FG	*GW*	LA			
49102	(44083)	p **GW**	FG	*GW*	LA			
49103	(44097)	p **GW**	FG	*GW*	LA			
49104	(44101)	p **GW**	FG	*GW*	LA			
49105	(44090)	p **GW**	FG	*GW*	LA			
49106	(44033)	p **GW**	A	*GW*	LA			
49107	(44064)	p **GW**	A	*GW*	LA			

49108	( )	**GW**			
49109	( )	**GW**			
49110	( )	**GW**			
49111	( )	**GW**			
49112	(44079)	p **GW**	FG	*GW*	LA
49113	( )	**GW**			

HST SET FORMATIONS

GREAT WESTERN RAILWAY

Great Western Railway withdrew its last full length HST sets in spring 2019. The company is retaining and refurbishing 11 4-car sets for use on regional and local services in the South-West. Until the refurbishment of these (which includes sliding doors) is completed a number of unrefurbished sets with slam doors have also still been retained. This includes two 5-car sets which are sub-leased to Hull Trains to provide cover for its Class 180 fleet.

Number of sets: 16 (at the time of writing). **Formations:** 4- or 5-cars.
Allocation: Laira (Plymouth) or St Philip's Marsh (Bristol).
Other maintenance and servicing depots: Long Rock (Penzance).
Operation: Principally Bristol–Exeter–Plymouth–Penzance and Cardiff–Bristol–Taunton.

Set	*D*	*C*	*B*	*A*	
LA21	42087	42364	42095	44042	
LA22	42566	42302	42304	44068	
LA23	42565	42103	42167	44100	
LA24	42582	42092	42016	44076	
LA25	42570	42310	42231	44069	
LA26	42563	42105	42580	44081	
LA72	42005	42176	42015	44005	

On sub-lease to Hull Trains

LA31	41166	40900	42347	42506	44002
LA32	41167	40902	42024	42026	44034

Spares:

LA:	40904	41160	42094	42175	42554

Power door fitted sets. 11 4-car sets being refurbished for continued use on local and regional services. GW01–GW07 completed at the time of writing.

Set	D	C	B	A
GW01	48103	48102	48101	49101
GW02	48106	48105	48104	49102
GW03	48109	48108	48107	49103
GW04	48112	48111	48110	49104
GW05	48115	48114	48113	49105
GW06	48118	48117	48116	49106
GW07	48121	48120	48119	49107
GW08	48124	48123	48122	49108
GW09	48127	48126	48125	49109
GW10	48130	48129	48128	49110
GW11	48133	48132	48131	49111

Spares:

LA:	48134	48135	49112	49113

LONDON NORTH EASTERN RAILWAY

LNER operates 15 HST sets on the ECML, but they are to be stored by the end of 2019. As well as serving non-electrified destinations such as Aberdeen and Inverness they also work alongside Class 91s and Mark 4 sets on services to Leeds, Newcastle and Edinburgh. Sets EC64 and NL65 transferred from East Midlands Trains in 2011 and 2015.

Number of sets: 15.
Maximum number of daily diagrams: 13.
Formations: 9-cars.
Allocation: Craigentinny (Edinburgh).
Other maintenance depot: Neville Hill (Leeds).
Operation: London King's Cross–Leeds/Harrogate/Lincoln/Newcastle/Edinburgh/Stirling/Aberdeen/Inverness.

Set	M	L	J	G	F	E	D	C	B
EC51	41120	41150	40748	42215	42091	42146	42150	42154	44094
EC52	41039	41040	40735	42323	42189	42057	42058	42059	44019
EC53	41090	41044	40737	42340	42127	42063	42064	42065	44045
EC54	41087	41088	40706	42104	42161	42171	42172	42219	44056
EC55	41091	41092	40704	42179	42188	42180	42181	42106	44058
EC56	41170	41118	40720	42241	42363	42242	42243	42244	44098
EC57	41151	41152	40740	42226	42128	42182	42186	42190	44080
EC58	41097	41098	40750	42158	42238	42191	42192	42193	44061
EC59	41099	41100	40711	42235	42239	42240	42198	42199	44063
EC60	41066	41164	40742	42355	42116	42357	42134	42122	44031
EC61	41115	41165	40702	42117	42159	42160	42109	42110	44057
EC62	41185	41095	40701	42306	42326	42330	42237	42307	44075
EC63	41159	41083	40708	42163	42286	42228	42130	42222	44050
EC64	41062	41154	40705	42125	42335	42123	42205	42210	44073
NL65	41112	41068	40805		42194	42229	42227	42225	44027

Spares:

EC:	40732	41190	42354	44077

EAST MIDLANDS RAILWAY

East Midlands Railway HSTs are concentrated on the St Pancras–Nottingham corridor during the day, with early morning and evening services to Leeds for servicing at Neville Hill.

The three 6-car sets were transferred from Grand Central at the end of 2017, entering traffic in spring 2018.

Number of sets: 12.   **Maximum number of daily diagrams:** 10.
Formations: 8-cars or 6-cars.
Allocation: Neville Hill (Leeds) or Derby Etches Park.
Operation: London St Pancras–Nottingham, Sheffield/Leeds.

Set	J	G	F	E	D	C	B	A
NL01	41057	41084	40730	42327	42111	42112	42113	44041
NL03	41061	41067	40741	42337	42119	42120	42121	44054
NL04	41077	41064	40749	42151	42164	42165	42153	44047
NL06	41156	41041	40746	42132	42131	42331	42133	44046
NL07	41111	41070	40754	42339	42135	42136	42137	44044
NL08	41071	41072	40753	42329	42139	42140	42141	44048
NL10	41075	41076	40756	42328	42341	42148	42149	44051
NL11	41117	41046	40728	42220	42100	42230	42124	44085
NL12	41079	41069	40700	42155	42156	42157	42152	44070
DY21	41207	40204	41204	42584	42402	42401		
DY22	41208	40205	41205	42585	42404	42405		
DY23	41209	40221	41206	42586	42407	42408		

Spares:

NL: 40751   41063   41113   42384   44071

CROSSCOUNTRY

CrossCountry HSTs run in 7-car formation with the spare TS coaches regularly used in traffic as coaches "C", "D" or "E". Sets are currently being fitted with sliding doors.

Number of sets: 5.   **Maximum number of daily diagrams:** 4.
Formations: 7-cars.   **Allocation:** Laira (Plymouth).
Other maintenance depots: Neville Hill (Leeds) or Edinburgh (Craigentinny).
Operation: Edinburgh–Leeds–Plymouth is the core route with some services extending to Dundee or Penzance.

Set	A	B	C	D	E	F	G	
XC01	41193	45001	42342	42097	42377	42374	44021	Refurbished
XC02	41194	45002	42372	42368	42373	42371	44072	
XC03	41195	45003	42370	42378	42036	42376	44052	Refurbished
XC04	41026	45004	42375	42369	42051	42366	44012	Refurbished
XC05	41035	45005	42290	42038	42053	42379	44017	

Spares:

LA: 42037   42052   42234   42367   42380

SCOTRAIL

ScotRail is introducing refurbished HSTs onto its Edinburgh/Glasgow–Aberdeen/Inverness services – branded INTER-7-CITY as they will serve Scotland's seven cities. There will ultimately be 17 5-car and nine 4-car sets but the refurbishment programme has been running behind schedule. As a result ScotRail introduced some unrefurbished sets into service. These will steadily be withdrawn as more sets are refurbished and fitted with sliding doors. At the time of writing all sets are running as 4-cars, 5-car sets are to be introduced in 2020.

Number of sets: 26 (by late 2020).
Formations: 4-cars or 5-cars.
Allocation: Power cars: Haymarket (Edinburgh), Trailers: Inverness.
Operation: Edinburgh/Glasgow–Aberdeen, Edinburgh/Glasgow–Inverness, Aberdeen–Inverness.

Set	A	B	C	D	
HA01	41124	42256	42255	44029	
HA02	41144	42295	42032	44039	
HA03	41104	42208	42206	44066	
HA04	41130	42325	42267	44032	
HA05	41022	42030	42010	44010	
HA06	41158	42200	42129	44086	
HA07	41010	42209	42069	44004	
HA10	41135	42279	42280	44035	
HA11	41136	42207	42047	44015	
HA18	40624	42265	42553	42293	Refurbished
HA19	40625	42259	42578	42333	Refurbished
HA20	40616	42291	42577	42075	Refurbished
HA21	40612	42055	42576	42276	Refurbished
HA22	40608	42275	42571	42019	Refurbished
HA23	40605	42345	42034	42184	Refurbished
HA24	40604	42183	42559	42343	Refurbished
HA25	40602	42292	42562	42045	Refurbished
HA26	40601	42004	42561	42046	Refurbished
HA31	41126	42344	42261	44030	
HA32	46010	42013	42012	44023	
HA33	41140	42287	42289	44037	

Spares:
IS: 42076 42118 42269 42301 42572 42579

3. SALOONS

Several specialist passenger carrying carriages, normally referred to as saloons are permitted to run on the national railway system. Many of these are to pre-nationalisation designs.

WCJS FIRST CLASS SALOON

Built 1892 by LNWR, Wolverton. Originally dining saloon mounted on six-wheel bogies. Rebuilt with new underframe with four-wheel bogies in 1927. Rebuilt 1960 as observation saloon with DMU end. Gangwayed at other end. The interior has a saloon, kitchen, guards vestibule and observation lounge. 19/– 1T. Gresley bogies. 28.5 t. 75 mph. ETS x.

| 41 | (484, 45018) | x | **M** | WC | *WC* | CS |

LNWR DINING SALOON

Built 1890 by LNWR, Wolverton. Mounted on the underframe of LMS General Utility Van 37908 in the 1980s. Contains kitchen and dining area seating 12 at tables for two. 12/–. Gresley bogies. 75 mph. 25.4 t. ETS x.

| 159 | (5159) | x | **M** | WC | *WC* | CS |

GNR FIRST CLASS SALOON

Built 1912 by GNR, Doncaster. Contains entrance vestibule, lavatory, two separate saloons, library and luggage space. 19/– 1T. Gresley bogies. 75 mph. 29.4 t. ETS x.

Non-standard livery: Teak.

| 807 | (4807) | x | **O** | WC | *WC* | CS |

LNER GENERAL MANAGERS SALOON

Built 1945 by LNER, York. Gangwayed at one end with a veranda at the other. The interior has a dining saloon seating 12, kitchen, toilet, office and nine seat lounge. 21/– 1T. B4 bogies. 75 mph. 35.7 t. ETS 3.

| 1999 | (902260) | | **M** | WC | | CS | DINING CAR No. 2 |

GENERAL MANAGER'S SALOON

Renumbered 1989 from London Midland Region departmental series. Formerly the LMR General Manager's saloon. Rebuilt from LMS period 1 Corridor Brake First M5033M to dia 1654 and mounted on the underframe of BR suburban Brake Standard M43232. Screw couplings have been removed. B4 bogies. 100 mph. ETS 2X.

LMS Lot No. 326 Derby 1927. 27.5 t.

6320   (5033, DM 395707)   x   **M**   PR   *PR*   SK

SUPPORT CAR

Converted 199? from Courier vehicle converted from Mark 1 Corridor Brake Standard 1986–87. Toilet retained and former compartment area replaced with train manager's office, crew locker room, linen store and dry goods store. The former luggage area has been adapted for use as an engineers' compartment and workshop. B5 bogies. 100 mph. ETS 2.

Lot No. 30721 Wolverton 1963. 35.5 t.

99545 (35466, 80207)   **PC**   BE   *BP*   SL   BAGGAGE CAR No. 11

SERVICE CAR

Converted from BR Mark 1 Corridor Brake Standard. Commonwealth bogies. 100 mph. ETS 2.

Lot No. 30721 Wolverton 1963.

99886 (35407)   x   **M**   WC   *WC*   CS   86   SERVICE CAR No. 1

ROYAL SCOTSMAN SALOONS

Built 1960 by Metro-Cammell as Pullman Kitchen Second for East Coast Main Line Services. Rebuilt 2016 as a Spa Car with two large bedrooms with bathroom/spa areas. Commonwealth bogies. xx t. ETS ?.

99337 (CAR No. 337)   **M**   BE   *RS*   ZG   STATE SPA CAR

Built 1960 by Metro-Cammell as Pullman Kitchen First for East Coast Main Line services. Rebuilt 2013 as dining car. Commonwealth bogies. 38.5 t. ETS ?.

99960 (321 SWIFT)   **M**   BE   *RS*   ZG   DINING CAR No. 2

Built 1960 by Metro-Cammell as Pullman Parlour First (§ Pullman Kitchen First) for East Coast Main Line services. Rebuilt 1990 as sleeping cars with four twin sleeping rooms (*§ three twin sleeping rooms and two single sleeping rooms at each end). Commonwealth bogies. 38.5 t. ETS ?.

99961	(324 AMBER) *	**M**	BE	*RS*	ZG	STATE CAR No. 1
99962	(329 PEARL)	**M**	BE	*RS*	ZG	STATE CAR No. 2
99963	(331 TOPAZ)	**M**	BE	*RS*	ZG	STATE CAR No. 3
99964	(313 FINCH) §	**M**	BE	*RS*	ZG	STATE CAR No. 4

Built 1960 by Metro-Cammell as Pullman Kitchen First for East Coast Main Line services. Rebuilt 1990 as observation car with open verandah seating 32. B4 bogies. 36.95 t. ETS ?.

| 99965 | (319 SNIPE) | **M** | BE | *RS* | ZG | OBSERVATION CAR |

Built 1960 by Metro-Cammell as Pullman Kitchen First for East Coast Main Line services. Rebuilt 1993 as dining car. Commonwealth bogies. 38.5 t. ETS ?.

| 99967 | (317 RAVEN) | **M** | BE | *RS* | ZG | DINING CAR No. 1 |

Mark 3A. Converted 1997 from a Sleeping Car at Carnforth Railway Restoration & Engineering Services. BT10 bogies. Attendant's and adjacent two sleeping compartments converted to generator room containing a 160 kW Volvo unit. In 99968 four sleeping compartments remain for staff use with another converted for use as a staff shower and toilet. The remaining five sleeping compartments have been replaced by two passenger cabins. In 99969 seven sleeping compartments remain for staff use. A further sleeping compartment, along with one toilet, have been converted to store rooms. The other two sleeping compartments have been combined to form a crew mess. 41.5 t. 99968 ETS index ?. 99969 ETS 7X (when generator not in use). ETS index ?? (when generator in use).

Lot No. 30960 Derby 1981–83.

| 99968 | (10541) | **M** | BE | *RS* | ZG | STATE CAR No. 5 |
| 99969 | (10556) | **M** | BE | *RS* | ZG | SERVICE CAR |

"CLUB CAR"

Converted from BR Mark 1 Open Standard at Carnforth Railway Restoration & Engineering Services in 1994. Contains kitchen, pantry and two dining saloons. 20/– 1T. Commonwealth bogies. 100 mph. ETS 4.

Lot No. 30724 York 1963. 37 t.

| 99993 | (5067) | x | **CC** | LS | *LS* | CL | CLUB CAR |

BR INSPECTION SALOON

Mark 1. Short frames. Non-gangwayed. Observation windows at each end. The interior layout consists of two saloons interspersed by a central lavatory/kitchen/guards/luggage section. 90 mph. ETS x.

BR Wagon Lot No. 3095 Swindon 1957. B4 bogies. 30.5 t.

| 999506 | | **M** | WC | *WC* | CS | |

4. PULLMAN CAR COMPANY SERIES

Pullman cars have never generally been numbered as such, although many have carried numbers, instead they have carried titles. However, a scheme of schedule numbers exists which generally lists cars in chronological order. In this section those numbers are shown followed by the car's title. Cars described as "kitchen" contain a kitchen in addition to passenger accommodation and have gas cooking unless otherwise stated. Cars described as "parlour" consist entirely of passenger accommodation. Cars described as "brake" contain a compartment for the use of the guard and a luggage compartment in addition to passenger accommodation.

PULLMAN PARLOUR FIRST

Built 1927 by Midland Carriage & Wagon Company. 26/– 2T. Gresley bogies. 41 t. ETS 2.

| 213 | MINERVA | PC | BE | BP | SL |

PULLMAN KITCHEN FIRST

Built 1928 by Metropolitan Carriage & Wagon Company. 20/– 1T. Gresley bogies. 42 t. ETS 4.

| 238 | PHYLISS | PC | BE | | SL |

PULLMAN PARLOUR FIRST

Built 1928 by Metropolitan Carriage & Wagon Company. 24/– 2T. Gresley bogies. 40 t. ETS 4.

| 239 | AGATHA | PC | BE | | SL |
| 243 | LUCILLE | PC | BE | BP | SL |

PULLMAN KITCHEN FIRST

Built 1925 by BRCW. Rebuilt by Midland Carriage & Wagon Company in 1928. 20/– 1T. Gresley bogies. 41 t. ETS 4.

| 245 | IBIS | PC | BE | BP | SL |

PULLMAN PARLOUR FIRST

Built 1928 by Metropolitan Carriage & Wagon Company. 24/– 2T. Gresley bogies. ETS 4.

| 254 | ZENA | PC | BE | BP | SL |

PULLMAN KITCHEN FIRST

Built 1928 by Metropolitan Carriage & Wagon Company. 20/– 1T. Gresley
bogies. 42 t. ETS 4.

| 255 | IONE | **PC** | BE | *BP* | SL |

PULLMAN KITCHEN COMPOSITE

Built 1932 by Metropolitan Carriage & Wagon Company. Originally included
in 6-Pul EMU. Electric cooking. 12/16 1T. EMU bogies. ETS x.

| 264 | RUTH | **PC** | BE | | SL |

PULLMAN KITCHEN FIRST

Built 1932 by Metropolitan Carriage & Wagon Company. Originally included
in "Brighton Belle" EMUs but now used as hauled stock. Electric cooking.
20/– 1T. B5 (SR) bogies (§ EMU bogies). 44 t. ETS 2.

280	AUDREY		**PC**	BE	*BP*	SL
281	GWEN		**PC**	BE	*BP*	SL
283	MONA	§	**PC**	BE		SL
284	VERA		**PC**	BE	*BP*	SL

PULLMAN PARLOUR THIRD

Built 1932 by Metropolitan Carriage & Wagon Company. Originally included
in "Brighton Belle" EMUs. –/56 2T. EMU bogies. ETS x.

Non-standard livery: BR Revised Pullman (blue & white lined out in white).

| 286 | CAR No. 86 | **0** | BE | | SL |

PULLMAN BRAKE THIRD

Built 1932 by Metropolitan Carriage & Wagon Company. Originally driving
motor cars in "Brighton Belle" EMUs. Traction and control equipment
removed for use as hauled stock. –/48 1T. EMU bogies. ETS x.

| 292 | CAR No. 92 | **PC** | BE | | SL |
| 293 | CAR No. 93 | **PC** | BE | | SL |

PULLMAN PARLOUR FIRST

Built 1951 by Birmingham Railway Carriage & Wagon Company. 32/– 2T.
Gresley bogies. 39 t. ETS 3.

| 301 | PERSEUS | **PC** | BE | *BP* | SL |

Built 1952 by Pullman Car Company, Preston Park using underframe and
bogies from 176 RAINBOW, the body of which had been destroyed by fire.
26/– 2T. Gresley bogies. 38 t. ETS 4.

| 302 | PHOENIX | **PC** | BE | *BP* | SL |

PULLMAN PARLOUR FIRST

Built 1951 by Birmingham Railway Carriage & Wagon Company. 32/– 2T. Gresley bogies. 39 t. ETS 3.

| 308 | CYGNUS | | **PC** | BE | *BP* | SL |

PULLMAN BAR FIRST

Built 1951 by Birmingham Railway Carriage & Wagon Company. Rebuilt 1999 by Blake Fabrications, Edinburgh with original timber-framed body replaced by a new fabricated steel body. Contains kitchen, bar, dining saloon and coupé. Electric cooking. 14/– 1T. Gresley bogies. ETS 3.

| 310 | PEGASUS | x | **PC** | LS | *LS* | CL |

Also carries "THE TRIANON BAR" branding.

PULLMAN PARLOUR FIRST

Built 1960–61 by Metro-Cammell for East Coast Main Line services. –/36 2T. Commonwealth bogies. 38.5 t. ETS x.

| 325 | AMBER | x | **PC** | WC | *WC* | CS |
| 326 | EMERALD | x | **PC** | WC | *WC* | CS |

PULLMAN KITCHEN SECOND

Built 1960–61 by Metro-Cammell for East Coast Main Line services. Commonwealth bogies. –/30 1T. 40 t. ETS x.

| 335 | CAR No. 335 | x | **PC** | VT | *VT* | TM |

PULLMAN PARLOUR SECOND

Built 1960–61 by Metro-Cammell for East Coast Main Line services. 347 is used as an Open First. –/42 2T. Commonwealth bogies. 38.5 t. ETS x.

347	CAR No. 347	x	**M**	WC	*WC*	CS
348	TOPAZ	x	**PC**	WC	*WC*	CS
349	CAR No. 349	x	**PC**	VT	*VT*	TM
350	TANZANITE	x	**PC**	WC	*WC*	CS
351	SAPPHIRE	x	**PC**	WC	*WC*	CS
352	AMETHYST	x	**PC**	WC	*WC*	CS
353	CAR No. 353	x	**PC**	VT		TM

PULLMAN SECOND BAR

Built 1960–61 by Metro-Cammell for East Coast Main Line services. –/24+17 bar seats. Commonwealth bogies. 38.5 t. ETS x.

| 354 | THE HADRIAN BAR | x | **PC** | WC | *WC* | CS |

5. LOCOMOTIVE SUPPORT CARRIAGES

These carriages have been adapted from Mark 1s and Mark 2s for use as support carriages for heritage steam and diesel locomotives. Some seating is retained for the use of personnel supporting the locomotives operation with the remainder of the carriage adapted for storage, workshop, dormitory and catering purposes. These carriages can spend considerable periods of time off the national railway system when the locomotives they support are not being used on that system. No owner or operator details are included in this section. After the depot code, the locomotive(s) each carriage is usually used to support is given.

CORRIDOR BRAKE FIRST

Mark 1. Commonwealth bogies. ETS 2.

14007. Lot No. 30382 Swindon 1959. 35 t.
17025. Lot No. 30718 Swindon 1963. Metal window frames. 36 t.

14007	(14007, 17007)	x	**M**	NY	LNER 61264
17025	(14025)	v	**M**	CS	LMS 45690

CORRIDOR BRAKE FIRST

Mark 2A. Pressure ventilated. B4 bogies. ETS 4.

14060. Lot No. 30775 Derby 1967–68. 32 t.
17096. Lot No. 30786 Derby 1968. 32 t.

14060	(14060, 17060)	v	**M**	TM	LMS 45596	
17096	(14096)		**PC**	SL	SR 35028	MERCATOR

CORRIDOR BRAKE COMPOSITE

Mark 1. ETS 2.

21096. Lot No. 30185 Metro-Cammell 1956. BR Mark 1 bogies. 32.5 t.
21232. Lot No. 30574 GRCW 1960. B4 bogies. 34 t.
21249. Lot No. 30669 Swindon 1961–62. Commonwealth bogies. 36 t.

21096	x	**M**	NY	LNER 60007
21232	x	**M**	SK	LMS 46201
21249	x	**CC**	SL	New Build 60163

CORRIDOR BRAKE STANDARD

Mark 1. Metal window frames and melamine interior panelling. ETS 2.

35317/322. Lot No. 30699 Wolverton 1962–63. Commonwealth bogies. 37 t.
35451–486. Lot No. 30721 Wolverton 1963. Commonwealth bogies. 37 t.

35317	x	**CC**	CL	Locomotives Services Crewe-based locomotives
35322	x	**M**	CS	WCRC Carnforth-based locomotives
35451	x	**CC**	CL	Locomotives Services Crewe-based locomotives
35461	x	**CH**	CL	GWR 5029
35463	v	**M**	CS	WCRC Carnforth-based locomotives
35468	x	**M**	YK	National Railway Museum locomotives
35470	v	**CH**	TM	Tyseley Locomotive Works-based locos
35476	x	**M**	SK	LMS 46233
35479	v	**M**	SH	LNER 61306
35486	x	**M**	TN	LNER 60009

CORRIDOR BRAKE FIRST

Mark 2C. Pressure ventilated. Renumbered when declassified. B4 bogies. ETS 4.

Lot No. 30796 Derby 1969–70. 32.5 t.

35508 (14128, 17128)	**M**	BQ	LMS 44871/45212/45407

CORRIDOR BRAKE FIRST

Mark 2A. Pressure ventilated. Renumbered when declassified. B4 bogies. ETS 4.

Lot No. 30786 Derby 1968. 32 t.

35517 (14088, 17088)	b	**M**	BQ	LMS 44871/45212/45407
35518 (14097, 17097)	b	**G**	CS	SR 34067

COURIER VEHICLE

Mark 1. Converted 1986–87 from Corridor Brake Standards. ETS 2.

80204/217. Lot No. 30699 Wolverton 1962. Commonwealth bogies. 37 t.
80220. Lot No. 30573 Gloucester 1960. B4 bogies. 33 t.

80204 (35297)	**M**	CS	WCRC Carnforth-based locomotives
80217 (35299)	**M**	CS	WCRC Carnforth-based locomotives
80220 (35276)	**M**	NY	LNER 62005

6. 95xxx & 99xxx RANGE NUMBER CONVERSION TABLE

The following table is presented to help readers identify carriages which may still carry numbers in the 95xxx and 99xxx number ranges of the former private owner number series, which is no longer in general use.

9xxxx	BR No.	9xxxx	BR No.	9xxxx	BR No.
95402	Pullman 326	99350	Pullman 350	99673	550
99025	Pullman 325	99351	Pullman 351	99674	551
99035	35322	99352	Pullman 352	99675	552
99040	21232	99353	Pullman 353	99676	553
99041	35476	99354	Pullman 354	99677	586
99052	Saloon 41	99361	Pullman 335	99678	504
99121	3105	99371	3128	99679	506
99122	3106	99405	35486	99680	17102
99125	3113	99530	Pullman 301	99710	18767
99127	3117	99531	Pullman 302	99716 *	18808
99128	3130	99532	Pullman 308	99718	18862
99131	Saloon 1999	99534	Pullman 245	99721	18756
99241	35449	99535	Pullman 213	99723	35459
99302	13323	99536	Pullman 254	99880	Saloon 159
99304	21256	99537	Pullman 280	99881	Saloon 807
99311	1882	99539	Pullman 255	99883	2108
99312	35463	99541	Pullman 243	99885	2110
99319	17168	99543	Pullman 284	99887	2127
99326	4954	99546	Pullman 281	99953	35468
99327	5044	99547	Pullman 292	99966	34525
99328	5033	99548	Pullman 293	99970	Pullman 232
99329	4931	99670	546	99972	Pullman 318
99347	Pullman 347	99671	548	99973	324
99348	Pullman 348	99672	549	99974	Pullman 328
99349	Pullman 349				

* The number 99716 has also been applied to 3416 for filming purposes.

7. SET FORMATIONS

LNER MARK 4 SET FORMATIONS

The LNER Mark 4 sets generally run in fixed formations. Class 91 locomotives are positioned next to Coach B. Sets BN23–BN25/BN27–BN30 were withdrawn in 2019 and the whole fleet is due to be withdrawn by LNER by June 2020. Some coaches will be taken on by Transport for Wales.

Set	B	C	D	E	F	H	K	L	M	DVT
BN01	12207	12417	12415	12414	12307	10307	11298	11301	11401	82207
BN02	12232	12402	12450	12448	12302	10302	11299	11302	11402	82202
BN03	12201	12401	12459	12478	12301	10320	11277	11303	11403	82219
BN04	12202	12480	12421	12518	12327	10303	11278	11304	11404	82209
BN05	12209	12486	12520	12522	12300	10326	11219	11305	11405	82210
BN06	12208	12406	12420	12422	12313	10309	11279	11306	11406	82208
BN07	12231	12411	12405	12489	12329	10323	11280	11307	11407	82204
BN08	12205	12481	12485	12407	12328	10300	11229	11308	11408	82211
BN09	12230	12513	12483	12514	12308	10304	11281	11309	11409	82215
BN10	12214	12419	12488	12443	12305	10331	11282	11310	11410	82205
BN11	12203	12437	12436	12484	12315	10308	11283	11311	11411	82218
BN12	12212	12431	12404	12426	12330	10333	11284	11312	11412	82212
BN13	12228	12469	12430	12424	12311	10313	11285	11313	11413	82213
BN14	12229	12410	12526	12423	12312	10332	11201	11314	11414	82206
BN15	12226	12442	12409	12515	12309	10306	11286	11315	11415	82214
BN16	12213	12428	12445	12433	12304	10315	11287	11316	11416	82222
BN17	12223	12444	12427	12432	12303	10324	11288	11317	11417	82225
BN18	12215	12453	12468	12467	12324	10305	11289	11318	11418	82220
BN19	12211	12434	12400	12470	12310	10318	11290	11319	11419	82201
BN20	12224	12477	12439	12440	12326	10321	11241	11320	11420	82200
BN21	12222	12461	12441	12476	12323	10330	11244	11321	11421	82227
BN22	12210	12452	12460	12473	12316	10301	11291	11322	11422	82230
BN26	12220	12474	12465	12429	12325	10311	11295	11326	11426	82223
Spare	12200									82217
										82224

TRANSPENNINE EXPRESS MARK 5A SET FORMATIONS

These new coaches are used in fixed formations hauled by a Class 68 locomotive in push-pull mode, initially between Liverpool and Scarborough and will then be introduced onto the Manchester Airport–Redcar Central route in 2020.

Set	E	D	C	B	A
TP01	11501	12701	12702	12703	12801
TP02	11502	12704	12705	12706	12802
TP03	11503	12707	12708	12709	12803
TP04	11504	12710	12711	12712	12804
TP05	11505	12713	12714	12715	12805
TP06	11506	12716	12717	12718	12806
TP07	11507	12719	12720	12721	12807
TP08	11508	12722	12723	12724	12808
TP09	11509	12725	12726	12727	12809
TP10	11510	12728	12729	12730	12810
TP11	11511	12731	12732	12733	12811
TP12	11512	12734	12735	12736	12812
TP13	11513	12737	12738	12739	12813
Spare					12814

8. SERVICE STOCK

Carriages in this section are used for internal purposes within the railway industry, ie they do not generate revenue from outside the industry. Most are numbered in the former BR departmental number series.

BARRIER, ESCORT & TRANSLATOR VEHICLES

These vehicles are used to move multiple unit, HST and other vehicles around the national railway system.

HST Barrier Vehicles. Mark 1/2A. Renumbered from BR departmental series, or converted from various types. B4 bogies (* Commonwealth bogies).

Non-standard livery: 6340, 6344, 6346 All over dark blue.

6330. Mark 2A. Lot No. 30786 Derby 1968.
6336/38/44. Mark 1. Lot No. 30715 Gloucester 1962.
6340. Mark 1. Lot No. 30669 Swindon 1962.
6346. Mark 2A. Lot No. 30777 Derby 1967.
6348. Mark 1. Lot No. 30163 Pressed Steel 1957.

6330	(14084, 975629)		**FB**	A	*RO*	LR
6336	(81591, 92185)		**FB**	A	*GW*	LA
6338	(81581, 92180)		**FB**	A	*RO*	LR
6340	(21251, 975678)	*	**0**	A	*RO*	LR
6344	(81263, 92080)		**0**	A	*RO*	LR
6346	(9422)		**0**	A	*LN*	EC
6348	(81233, 92963)		**FB**	A	*GW*	LA

Mark 4 Barrier Vehicles. Mark 2A. Converted from Corridor First. B4 bogies. Lot No. 30774 Derby 1968.

6352	(13465, 19465)	**HB**	E	*LN*	BN
6353	(13478, 19478)	**HB**	E	*LN*	BN

EMU Translator Vehicles. Mark 1. Converted 1980 from Restaurant Unclassified Opens. 6376/77 have Tightlock couplers and 6378/79 Dellner couplers. Commonwealth bogies.

Lot No. 30647 Wolverton 1959–61.

6376	(1021, 975973)	**PB**	P	*DB*	TO *(works with 6377)*
6377	(1042, 975975)	**PB**	P	*DB*	TO *(works with 6376)*
6378	(1054, 975971)	**PB**	P	*DB*	TO *(works with 6379)*
6379	(1059, 975972)	**PB**	P	*DB*	TO *(works with 6378)*

Brake Force Runners. Mark 1. Previously used as HST Barrier Vehicles. Converted from Gangwayed Brake Vans in 1994–95. B4 bogies.

6392. Lot No. 30715 Gloucester 1962.
6397. Lot No. 30716 Gloucester 1962.

6392	(81588, 92183)	**PB**	CS	*CS*	ZA
6397	(81600, 92190)	**PB**	CS	*CS*	ZA

HST Barrier Vehicles. Mark 1. Converted from Gangwayed Brake Vans in 1994–95. B4 bogies.

6393. Lot No. 30716 Gloucester 1962.
6394. Lot No. 30162 Pressed Steel 1956–57.
6398/99. Lot No. 30400 Pressed Steel 1957–58.

6393	(81609, 92196)	**PB**	P	*LN*	EC
6394	(80878, 92906)	**PB**	P	*LN*	EC
6398	(81471, 92126)	**PB**	EM	*EM*	NL
6399	(81367, 92994)	**PB**	EM	*EM*	NL

Escort Coaches. Converted from Mark 2A (* Mark 2E) Open Brake Standards. 9419/28 use the same bodyshell as the Mark 2A Corridor Brake First. B4 bogies.

9419. Lot No.30777 Derby 1970.
9428. Lot No.30820 Derby 1970.
9506/08. Lot No.30838 Derby 1972.

9419		**DS**	DR	*DR*	KM
9428		**DS**	DR	*DR*	KM
9506	*	**DS**	DR	*DR*	KM
9508	*	**DS**	DR	*DR*	KM

EMU Translator Vehicles. Converted from Class 508 driving cars.

64664. Lot No. 30979 York 1979–80.
64707. Lot No. 30981 York 1979–80.

64664	**AG**	A	*GB*	ZG	Liwet	*(works with 64707)*
64707	**AG**	A	*GB*	ZG	Labezerin	*(works with 64664)*

EMU Translator Vehicles. Converted from Class 489 DMLVs that had originally been Class 414/3 DMBSOs. Previously used as de-icing coaches.

Lot No. 30452 Ashford/Eastleigh 1959. Mk 4 bogies.

68501	(61281)	**AG**	AF	*RO*	LR
68504	(61286)	**AG**	AF	*RO*	LR

Eurostar Barrier Vehicles. Mark 1. Converted from General Utility Vans with bodies removed. Fitted with B4 bogies for use as Eurostar barrier vehicles.

96380/381. Lot No. 30417 Pressed Steel 1958–59.
96383. Lot No. 30565 Pressed Steel 1959.
96384. Lot No. 30616 Pressed Steel 1959–60.

96380	(86386, 6380)	**B**	EU	*EU*	TI
96381	(86187, 6381)	**B**	EU	*EU*	TI
96383	(86664, 6383)	**B**	EU	*EU*	TI
96384	(86955, 6384)	**B**	EU	*EU*	TI

Brake Force Runners. Converted from Motorail vans built 1998–99 by Marcroft Engineering using underframe and running gear from Motorail General Utility Vans. B5 bogies.

Lot No. 30417 Pressed Steel 1958–59.

96604	(86337, 96156)	**Y**	CS	*CS*	ZA
96606	(86324, 96213)	**Y**	CS	*CS*	ZA

96608	(86385, 96216)	**Y**	CS	*CS*	ZA	
96609	(86327, 96217)	**Y**	CS	*CS*	ZA	

EMU Translator Vehicles. Converted from various Mark 1s.

Non-standard livery: All over blue.

975864. Lot No. 30054 Eastleigh 1951–54. Commonwealth bogies.
975867. Lot No. 30014 York 1950–51. Commonwealth bogies.
975875. Lot No. 30143 Charles Roberts 1954–55. Commonwealth bogies.
975974/978. Lot No. 30647 Wolverton 1959–61. B4 bogies.
977087. Lot No. 30229 Metro-Cammell 1955–57. Commonwealth bogies.

975864	(3849)	**HB**	E		BU		*(works with 975867)*
975867	(1006)	**HB**	E		BU		*(works with 975864)*
975875	(34643)	**O**	E	*RO*	LR		*(works with 977087)*
975974	(1030)	**AG**	A	*GB*	ZG	Paschar	*(works with 975978)*
975978	(1025)	**AG**	A	*GB*	ZG	Perpetiel	*(works with 975974)*
977087	(34971)	**O**	E	*RO*	LR		*(works with 975875)*

LABORATORY, TESTING & INSPECTION COACHES

These coaches are used for research, testing and inspection on the national railway system. Many are fitted with sophisticated technical equipment.

Plain Line Pattern Recognition Coaches. Converted from BR Mark 2F Buffet First (*) or Open Standard. B4 bogies.

1256. Lot No. 30845 Derby 1973.
5981. Lot No. 30860 Derby 1973–74.

1256	(3296)	*	**Y**	NR	*CS*	ZA
5981			**Y**	NR	*CS*	ZA

Generator Vans. Mark 1. Converted from BR Mark 1 Gangwayed Brake Vans. B5 bogies.

6260. Lot No. 30400 Pressed Steel 1957–58.
6261. Lot No. 30323 Pressed Steel 1957.
6262. Lot No. 30228 Metro-Cammell 1957–58.
6263. Lot No. 30163 Pressed Steel 1957.
6264. Lot No. 30173 York 1956.

6260	(81450, 92116)	**Y**	NR	*CS*	ZA
6261	(81284, 92988)	**Y**	NR	*CS*	ZA
6262	(81064, 92928)	**Y**	NR	*CS*	ZA
6263	(81231, 92961)	**Y**	NR	*CS*	ZA
6264	(80971, 92923)	**Y**	NR	*CS*	ZA

Staff Coach. Mark 2D. Converted from BR Mark 2D Open Brake Standard. Lot No. 30824 Derby 1971. B4 bogies.

9481	**Y**	NR	*CS*	ZA

Test Train Brake Force Runners. Mark 2F. Converted from BR Mark 2F Open Brake Standard. Lot No. 30861 Derby 1974. B4 bogies.

9516	**Y**	NR	*CS*	ZA
9523	**Y**	NR	*CS*	ZA

Driving Trailer Coaches. Converted 2008 at Serco, Derby from Mark 2F Driving Open Brake Standards. Fitted with generator. Disc brakes. B4 bogies.

9701–08. Lot No. 30861 Derby 1974. Converted to Driving Open Brake Standard Glasgow 1974.

9714. Lot No. 30861 Derby 1974. Converted to Driving Open Brake Standard Glasgow 1986.

9701	(9528)	Y	NR	*CS*	ZA
9702	(9510)	Y	NR	*CS*	ZA
9703	(9517)	Y	NR	*CS*	ZA
9708	(9530)	Y	NR	*CS*	ZA
9714	(9536)	Y	NR	*CS*	ZA

Ultrasonic Test Coach. Converted from Class 421 EMU MBSO.

62287. Lot No. 30808. York 1970. SR Mark 6 bogies.

62384. Lot No. 30816. York 1970. SR Mark 6 bogies.

62287	Y	NR	*CS*	ZA
62384	Y	NR	*CS*	ZA

Test Train Brake Force Runners. Converted from Mark 2F Open Standard converted to Class 488/3 EMU TSOLH. These vehicles are included in test trains to provide brake force and are not used for any other purposes. Lot No. 30860 Derby 1973–74. B4 bogies.

72612	(6156)	Y	NR	*CS*	ZA
72616	(6007)	Y	NR	*CS*	ZA

Structure Gauging Train Coach. Converted from Mark 2F Open Standard converted to Class 488/3 EMU TSOLH. Lot No. 30860 Derby 1973–74. B4 bogies.

72630	(6094)	Y	NR	*CS*	ZA	*(works with 99666)*

Plain Line Pattern Recognition Coaches. Converted from BR Mark 2F Open Standard converted to Class 488/3 EMU TSOLH. Lot No. 30860 Derby 1973–74. B4 bogies.

72631	(6096)	Y	NR	*CS*	ZA
72639	(6070)	Y	NR	*CS*	ZA

Driving Trailer Coaches. Converted from Mark 3B 110 mph Driving Brake Vans. Fitted with diesel generator. Lot No. 31042 Derby 1988. T4 bogies.

82111	Y	NR	ZA
82124	Y	NR	ZA
82129	Y	NR	ZA
82145	Y	NR	ZA

Structure Gauging Train Coach. Converted from BR Mark 2E Open First then converted to exhibition van. Lot No. 30843 Derby 1972–73. B4 bogies.

99666	(3250)	Y	NR	ZA	*(works with 72630)*

Inspection Saloon. Converted from Class 202 DEMU TRB at Stewarts Lane for use as a BR Southern Region General Manager's Saloon. Overhauled at FM Rail, Derby 2004–05 for use as a New Trains Project Saloon. Can be used in push-pull mode with suitably equipped locomotives. Eastleigh 1958. SR Mark 4 bogies.

975025	(60755)	G	NR	*CS*	ZA	CAROLINE

Overhead Line Equipment Test Coach ("MENTOR"). Converted from BR Mark 1 Corridor Brake Standard. Lot No. 30142 Gloucester 1954–55. Fitted with pantograph. B4 bogies.

975091 (34615)   Y   NR   *CS*   ZA

New Measurement Train Conference Coach. Converted from prototype HST TF Lot No. 30848 Derby 1972. BT10 bogies.

975814 (11000, 41000)   Y   NR   *CS*   ZA

New Measurement Train Lecture Coach. Converted from prototype HST catering vehicle. Lot No. 30849 Derby 1972–73. BT10 bogies.

975984 (10000, 40000)   Y   NR   *CS*   ZA

Radio Survey Coach. Converted from BR Mark 2E Open Standard. Lot No. 30844 Derby 1972–73. B4 bogies.

977868 (5846)   Y   NR   *CS*   ZA

Staff Coach. Converted from Royal Household couchette Lot No. 30889, which in turn had been converted from BR Mark 2B Corridor Brake First. Lot No. 30790 Derby 1969. B5 bogies.

977969 (14112, 2906)   Y   NR   *CS*   ZA

Track Inspection Train Coach. Converted from BR Mark 2E Open Standard. Lot No. 30844 Derby 1972–73. B4 bogies.

977974 (5854)   Y   NR   *CS*   ZA

Electrification Measurement Coach. Converted from BR Mark 2F Open First converted to Class 488/2 EMU TFOH. Lot No. 30859 Derby 1973–74. B4 bogies.

977983 (3407, 72503)   Y   NR   *CS*   ZA

New Measurement Train Staff Coach. Converted from HST catering vehicle. Lot No. 30884 Derby 1976–77. BT10 bogies.

977984 (40501)   Y   P   *CS*   ZA

Structure Gauging Train Coaches. Converted from Mark 2F Open Standard converted to Class 488/3 EMU TSOLH or from BR Mark 2D Open First subsequently declassified to Open Standard and then converted to exhibition van. B4 bogies.

977985. Lot No. 30860 Derby 1973–74.
977986. Lot No. 30821 Derby 1971.

977985 (6019, 72715)   Y   NR   *CS*   ZA *(works with 977986)*
977986 (3189, 99664)   Y   NR   *CS*   ZA *(works with 977985)*

New Measurement Train Overhead Line Equipment Test Coach. Converted from HST TGS. Lot No. 30949 Derby 1982. Fitted with pantograph. BT10 bogies.

977993 (44053)   Y   P   *CS*   ZA

New Measurement Train Track Recording Coach. Converted from HST TGS. Lot No. 30949 Derby 1982. BT10 bogies.

977994 (44087)   Y   P   *CS*   ZA

New Measurement Train Coach. Converted from HST catering vehicle. Lot No. 30921 Derby 1978–79. Fitted with generator. BT10 bogies.

977995	(40719, 40619)	**Y**	P	*CS*	ZA

Radio Survey Coach. Converted from Mark 2F Open Standard converted to Class 488/3 EMU TSOLH. Lot No. 30860 Derby 1973–74. B4 bogies.

977997	(72613, 6126)	**Y**	NR	*CS*	ZA

Track Recording Coach. Purpose built Mark 2. BR Wagon Lot No. 3830 Derby 1976. B4 bogies.

999550		**Y**	NR	*CS*	ZA

Ultrasonic Test Coaches. Converted from Class 421 EMU MBSO and Class 432 EMU MSO.

999602/605. Lot No. 30862 York 1974. SR Mk 6 bogies.
999606. Lot No. 30816. York 1970. SR Mk 6 bogies.

999602	(62483)	**Y**	NR	*CS*	ZA
999605	(62482)	**Y**	NR	*CS*	ZA
999606	(62356)	**Y**	NR	*CS*	ZA

BREAKDOWN TRAIN COACHES

These coaches are formed in trains used for the recovery of derailed railway vehicles and were converted from BR Mark 1 Corridor Brake Standard and General Utility Van. The current use of each vehicle is given.

971001/003/004. Lot No. 30403 York/Glasgow 1958–60. Commonwealth bogies.
971002. Lot No. 30417 Pressed Steel 1958–59. Commonwealth bogies.
975087. Lot No. 30032 Wolverton 1951–52. BR Mark 1 bogies.
975464. Lot No. 30386 Charles Roberts 1956–58. Commonwealth bogies.
975471. Lot No. 30095 Wolverton 1953–55. Commonwealth bogies.
975477. Lot No. 30233 GRCW 1955–57. BR Mark 1 bogies.
975486. Lot No. 30025 Wolverton 1950–52. Commonwealth bogies.

971001	(86560, 94150)	**Y**	NR	*DB*	SP	Tool & Generator Van
971002	(86624, 94190)	**Y**	NR	*DB*	SP	Tool Van
971003	(86596, 94191)	**Y**	NR	*DB*	SP	Tool Van
971004	(86194, 94168)	**Y**	NR	*DB*	SP	Tool Van
975087	(34289)	**Y**	NR	*DB*	SP	Tool & Generator Van
975464	(35171)	**Y**	NR	*DB*	SP	Staff Coach
975471	(34543)	**Y**	NR	*DB*	SP	Staff Coach
975477	(35108)	**Y**	NR	*DB*	SP	Staff Coach
975486	(34100)	**Y**	NR	*DB*	SP	Tool & Generator Van

INFRASTRUCTURE MAINTENANCE COACH

Winterisation Train Coach. Converted from BR Mark 2E Open Standard. Lot No. 30844 Derby 1972–73. B4 bogies.

977869	(5858)	**Y**	NR	*DR*	Perth CS

INTERNAL USER VEHICLES

These vehicles are confined to yards and depots or do not normally move. Details are given of the internal user number (if allocated), type, former identity, current use and location. Many no longer see regular use. * = Grounded body.

975403 carries its original number 4598.

041474*	BR SPV 975418	Stores Van	Worksop Up Yard
041989*	BR SPV 975423	Stores Van	Toton Depot
042154	BR GUV 93975	Stores van	Ipswich Upper Yard
061202*	BR GUV 93498	Stores Van	Laira Depot, Plymouth
–	BR NA 94322*	Stores Van	WCRC, Carnforth Depot
083602	BR CCT 94494	Stores van	Three Bridges Station
–	BR NB 94548*	Stores Van	WCRC, Carnforth Depot
083637	BR NW 99203	Stores Van	Stewarts Lane Depot
083644	BR Ferry Van 889201	Stores van	Eastleigh Depot
083664	BR Ferry Van 889203	Stores van	Eastleigh Depot
–	BR Open Standard 5636	Instruction Coach	St Philip's Marsh Depot
–	BR BV 6360	Barrier vehicle	Neville Hill Depot, Leeds
–	BR BV 6396	Stores van	Longsight Depot (Manchester)
–	BR RFKB 10256	Instruction Coach	Yoker Depot
–	BR RFKB 10260	Instruction Coach	Yoker Depot
–	BR SPV 88045*	Stores Van	Thames Haven Yard
–	BR NL 94003	Stores van	Burton-upon-Trent Depot
–	BR NK 94121	Stores van	Toton Depot
–	BR NB 94438	Stores van	Toton Depot
–	BR CCT 94663*	Stores van	Mossend Up Yard
–	BR GUV 96139	Stores van	Longsight Depot, Manchester
–	BR Ferry Van 889200	Stores van	Stewarts Lane Depot
–	BR Ferry Van 889202	Stores van	Stewarts Lane Depot
–	SR PMV 977045*	Stores Van	EMD, Longport Works
–	SR CCT 2516*	Stores Van	Eastleigh Depot

Abbreviations:

BV = Barrier Vehicle
CCT = Covered Carriage Truck (a 4-wheeled van similar to a GUV)
GUV = General Utility Van (bogied van with side and end doors)
NAA = Propelling Control Vehicle
NB = High Security Brake Van (converted from Gangwayed Brake Van, gangways removed)
NK = High Security General Utility Van (end doors removed)
NL = Newspaper Van (converted from a GUV)
NW = Bullion Van (converted from a Corridor Brake Standard)
PMV = Parcels & Miscellaneous Van (a 4-wheeled van similar to a CCT but without end doors)
RFKB = Kitchen Buffet First
SPV = Special Parcels Van (a 4-wheeled van converted from a Fish Van)

9. COACHING STOCK AWAITING DISPOSAL

This list shows the locations of carriages awaiting disposal. The definition of which vehicles are awaiting disposal is somewhat vague, but often these are vehicles of types not now in normal service, those not expected to see further use or that have originated from preservationists as a source of spares or possible future use or carriages which have been damaged by fire, vandalism or collision.

1201	TM	3336	DE	5777	BU	9440	SH
1252	SH	3351	TM	5797	RO	9489	CS
1253	SH	3358	BU	5815	SH	9490	BU
1258	CS	3368	FA	5876	SH	9496	DE
1644	CS	3379	DE	5888	SH	9529	DR
1650	CS	3388	FA	5922	DR	9531	DR
1652	CS	3399	FA	5924	DR	10237	LM
1655	CS	3400	BU	5925	SH	10242	LM
1658	CL	3408	CS	5928	TM	10245	CS
1663	CS	3416	TM	5943	CS	10530	ZN
1670	CS	3417	DE	5954	ME	10578	ZN
1679	RO	3424	BU	5958	SH	10588	ZN
1696	CL	4362	BU	5959	DR	10656	ZN
1800	SH	4796	BU	5978	SH	11006	BU
1883	CL	4799	BU	6009	SH	11021	LM
1954	CL	4849	CS	6029	SH	11033	LM
2108	CS	4860	CS	6036	DR	11079	LM
2110	CS	4932	CS	6041	CS	11097	LM
2127	CS	4997	CS	6045	SH	12096	ZN
2131	CS	5027	BU	6050	CS	12104	LM
2833	CS	5054	RO	6073	SH	12165	LM
2909	CS	5179	TM	6110	ME	13306	CS
3045	CL	5183	TM	6134	SH	13323	CS
3051	CL	5186	TM	6139	ME	13508	RO
3060	CL	5194	TM	6151	SH	17013	CL
3091	RO	5331	FA	6152	DR	17168	CS
3107	RO	5386	FA	6154	SH	18767	SH
3140	RO	5420	TM	6175	CS	18808	SH
3241	CS	5453	CS	6179	CS	18862	CS
3255	FA	5463	CS	6324	CP	21268	RO
3277	RO	5478	CS	6351	BU	34525	CS
3279	BU	5491	CS	6361	NL	35333	ZG
3292	BU	5569	CS	6364	CF	35467	CL
3295	RO	5631	ME	6365	CF	68505	ZG
3303	TO	5657	BU	6412	CL	80212	CS
3309	TM	5710	ZM	6720	FA	80374	BU
3318	BU	5737	CS	6722	LM	80403	CS
3331	BU	5740	CS	7204	CL	80404	CS
3334	DE	5756	CS	7931	BU	80414	SL

82101	LW	94316	TO	94504	Hellifield	96373	LM
82115	ZN	94317	TO	94512	CS	96374	ZB
82126	LW	94323	Hellifield	94515	ZG	96375	LM
82138	LM	94326	Hellifield	94517	BU	96602	Barry
82150	LM	94332	CS	94520	BU	96603	CF
92114	ZA	94333	Hellifield	94522	CL	96605	Barry
92159	CS	94335	CL	94525	CS	96607	Barry
92908	CS	94336	CL	94526	CS	99019	CS
93723	BY	94337	WE	94527	Hellifield	99884	CL
94058	BU	94338	WE	94530	CS	975081	BU
94101	CS	94344	TO	94531	BU	975280	BU
94104	TO	94401	CS	94538	CL	975454	TO
94106	BU	94406	CS	94539	CS	975484	CS
94116	BU	94408	CS	94540	TJ	975490	BU
94153	WE	94410	WE	94542	CS	975639	CS
94166	BU	94420	CS	94545	HM	975681	Portobello
94170	CL	94422	TO	94546	Hellifield	975682	Portobello
94176	BU	94423	BU	94547	CS	975685	Portobello
94177	TO	94427	WE	95300	CS	975686	Portobello
94195	BU	94428	CS	95410	CS	975687	Portobello
94196	CS	94429	HM	95727	WE	975688	Portobello
94197	BU	94431	CS	95754	CS	975920	Portobello
94207	TO	94434	CL	95761	WE	977085	BU
94208	TO	94435	TO	95763	BU	977095	CS
94214	CS	94445	WE	96110	CS	977169	BU
94222	CS	94450	WE	96132	CS	977241	BU
94227	HM	94451	WE	96135	CS	977450	BU
94229	CL	94470	TO	96164	CS	977618	BY
94302	Hellifield	94479	TO	96165	CS	999509	CL
94303	Hellifield	94482	CS	96170	CS	083439	BU
94304	MH	94488	BU	96178	CS		
94306	Hellifield	94490	BU	96182	CS	DS70220 Western	
94308	CS	94492	WE	96191	CS	Trading Estate	
94310	WE	94495	Hellifield	96192	CS	Siding, North Acton	
94311	WE	94498	CS	96371	LR	Pullman 315 CS	
94313	WE	94501	TO	96372	LM	Pullman 316 HN	

10. CODES

10.1. LIVERY CODES

The colour of the lower half of the bodyside is stated first. Minor variations to these liveries are ignored.

AG Arlington Fleet Services (green).
AL Advertising/promotional livery (see class heading for details).
AR Anglia Railways (turquoise blue with a white stripe).
AV Arriva Trains (turquoise blue with white doors).
AW Arriva Trains Wales/Welsh Government sponsored dark & light blue.
B BR blue.
BG BR blue & grey lined out in white.
CA Caledonian Sleeper (dark blue).
CC BR Carmine & Cream.
CH BR Western Region/GWR chocolate & cream lined out in gold.
CM Chiltern Railways Mainline (two-tone grey/white & silver with blue stripes).
DR Direct Rail Services (dark blue with light blue or dark grey roof).
DS Revised Direct Rail Services (dark blue, light blue & green. Compass logo).
EA East Midlands Trains revised HST (dark blue, orange & red).
FB First Group dark blue.
FD First Great Western "Dynamic Lines" (dark blue with thin multi-coloured lines on lower bodyside).
FS First Group (indigo blue with pink & white stripes).
G BR Southern Region/SR green.
GA Greater Anglia (white with red doors & black window surrounds).
GC Grand Central (black with an orange stripe).
GW Great Western Railway (TOC) dark green.
HB HSBC Rail (Oxford blue & white)
IC BR InterCity (light grey/red stripe/white stripe/dark grey).
M BR maroon (maroon lined out in straw & black).
O Non-standard (see class heading for details).
PB Porterbrook Leasing Company (blue).
PC Pullman Car Company (umber & cream with gold lettering lined out in gold).
RB Riviera Trains Oxford blue.
RP Royal Train (claret, lined out in red & black).
RV Riviera Trains Great Briton (Oxford blue & cream, lined out in gold).
SI ScotRail InterCity (light grey & dark blue with INTER7CITY branding).
SR ScotRail – Scotland's Railways (dark blue with Scottish Saltire flag & white/blue flashes).
ST Stagecoach {long-distance stock} (white & dark blue with dark blue window surrounds and red & orange swishes at unit ends).
TP TransPennine Express (silver, grey, blue & purple).
V Virgin Trains (red with black doors extending into bodysides, three white lower bodyside stripes).
VE Virgin Trains East Coast (red & white with black window surrounds).

VN	Northern Belle (crimson lake & cream lined out in gold).
VT	Virgin Trains silver (silver, with black window surrounds, white cantrail stripe and red roof. Red swept down at unit ends).
XC	CrossCountry (two tone silver with deep crimson ends & pink doors).
Y	Network Rail yellow.

10.2. OWNER CODES

The following codes are used to define the ownership details of the rolling stock listed in this book. Codes shown indicate either the legal owner or "responsible custodian" of each vehicle.

A	Angel Trains
AF	Arlington Fleet Services
AV	Arriva UK Trains
BE	Belmond (UK)
BN	Beacon Rail
CA	Caledonian Sleepers Rail Leasing
CS	Colas Rail
DB	DB Cargo (UK)
DR	Direct Rail Services
E	Eversholt Rail (UK)
EA	Eastern Rail Services
EM	East Midlands Railway
EU	Eurostar (UK)
FG	First Group
LF	Lombard Finance
LS	Locomotive Services
LU	London Underground
NN	North Norfolk Railway
NR	Network Rail
NY	North Yorkshire Moors Railway Enterprises
P	Porterbrook Leasing Company
PR	The Princess Royal Class Locomotive Trust
RP	Rampart Engineering
RV	Riviera Trains
SP	The Scottish Railway Preservation Society
VT	Vintage Trains
WC	West Coast Railway Company

10.3. OPERATOR CODES

The two letter operator codes give the current operator (by trading name). This is the organisation which facilitates the use of the coach and may not be the actual Train Operating Company which runs the train on which the particular coach is used. If no operator code is shown then the vehicle is not in use at present.

BP	Belmond British Pullman
CA	Caledonian Sleeper

CR	Chiltern Railways
CS	Colas Rail
DB	DB Cargo (UK)
DR	Direct Rail Services
EM	East Midlands Trains
EU	Eurostar (UK)
GA	Greater Anglia
GB	GB Railfreight
GC	Grand Central
GW	Great Western Railway
HT	Hull Trains
LN	London North Eastern Railway
LS	Locomotive Services (TOC)
NY	North Yorkshire Moors Railway
RO	Rail Operations Group
RS	The Royal Scotsman (Belmond)
RT	Royal Train
RV	Riviera Trains
SP	The Scottish Railway Preservation Society
SR	ScotRail
TP	TransPennine Express
TW	Transport for Wales
VT	Vintage Trains
WC	West Coast Railway Company
XC	CrossCountry

10.4. ALLOCATION & LOCATION CODES

Code	Depot	Depot Operator
AL	Aylesbury	Chiltern Railways
BN	Bounds Green (London)	London North Eastern Railway
BO	Bo'ness (West Lothian)	The Bo'ness & Kinneil Railway
BQ	Bury (Greater Manchester)	East Lancashire Railway Trust
BU	Burton-upon-Trent	Nemesis Rail
BY	Bletchley	West Midlands Trains
CF	Cardiff Canton	Transport for Wales/Colas Rail
CL	Crewe LNWR Heritage	LNWR Heritage Company
CP	Crewe Arriva TrainCare	Arriva TrainCare
CS	Carnforth	West Coast Railway Company
DE	East Dereham (Norfolk)	Mid Norfolk Railway
DR	Doncaster Belmont Yard	*Storage location only*
DY	Derby Etches Park	East Midlands Railway
EC	Edinburgh Craigentinny	London North Eastern Railway
EH	Eastleigh	Arriva TrainCare
EP	Ely Papworth Sidings	*Storage location only*
FA	Fawley (Hampshire)	*Storage location only*
HM	Healey Mills (Wakefield)	*Storage location only*
IL	Ilford (London)	Greater Anglia

IS	Inverness	ScotRail
KM	Carlisle Kingmoor	Direct Rail Services
LA	Laira (Plymouth)	Great Western Railway
LM	Quinton Rail Technology Centre (Long Marston, Warwickshire)	Motorail Logistics
LR	Leicester	UK Rail Leasing
LW	MoD Longtown (Cumbria)	*Storage location only*
MA	Longsight (Manchester)	Alstom
ME	Mossend Yard	*Storage location only*
MH	Millerhill (Edinburgh)	*Storage location only*
ML	Motherwell	Direct Rail Services
NC	Norwich Crown Point	Greater Anglia
NL	Neville Hill (Leeds)	East Midlands Railway/Northern
NO	Weybourne (Norfolk)	North Norfolk Railway
NY	Grosmont (North Yorkshire)	North Yorkshire Moors Railway Enterprises
PM	St Philip's Marsh (Bristol)	Great Western Railway
PO	Polmadie (Glasgow)	Alstom
PZ	Penzance Long Rock	Great Western Railway
RO	Rowsley (Derbyshire)	Peak Rail
RS	Ruislip (London)	London Underground
SH	Southall (London)	West Coast Railway Co/Locomotive Services
SK	Swanwick West (Derbyshire)	The Princess Royal Locomotive Trust
SL	Stewarts Lane (London)	Govia Thameslink Railway/Belmond
SP	Springs Branch (Wigan)	DB Cargo (UK)
TJ	Tavistock Junction Yard (Plymouth)	*Storage location only*
TI	Temple Mills (London)	Eurostar (UK)
TM	Tyseley Locomotive Works	Vintage Trains
TN	Thornton (Fife)	John Cameron
TO	Toton (Nottinghamshire)	DB Cargo (UK)
WE	Willesden Brent Sidings	*Storage location only*
WO	Wolsingham (Weardale Railway)	RMS Locotec
WS	Worksop (Nottinghamshire)	Harry Needle Railroad Company
YK	National Railway Museum (York)	National Museum of Science & Industry
ZA	RTC Business Park (Derby)	Loram (UK)
ZB	Doncaster Works	Wabtec Rail
ZC	Crewe Works	Bombardier Transportation UK
ZD	Derby Works	Bombardier Transportation UK
ZG	Eastleigh Works	Arlington Fleet Services
ZH	Springburn Depot (Glasgow)	*closed*
ZI	Ilford Works	Bombardier Transportation UK
ZJ	Stoke-on-Trent Works	Axiom Rail (Stoke)
ZK	Kilmarnock Caledonia Works	Wabtec Rail Scotland
ZM	Kilmarnock Bonnyton Works	Brodie Engineering
ZN	Wolverton Works	Knorr-Bremse Rail Systems (UK)
ZR	Holgate Works (York)	Network Rail